Wilmer Cave France Wright

The Emperor Julian's Relation to the New Sophistic and Neo-Platonism

Wilmer Cave France Wright

The Emperor Julian's Relation to the New Sophistic and Neo-Platonism

ISBN/EAN: 9783337005511

Printed in Europe, USA, Canada, Australia, Japan

Cover: Foto ©ninafisch / pixelio.de

More available books at **www.hansebooks.com**

THE EMPEROR JULIAN'S RELATION TO THE NEW SOPHISTIC AND NEO-PLATONISM: WITH A STUDY OF HIS STYLE

A DISSERTATION
PRESENTED TO THE FACULTY OF ARTS, LITERATURE
AND SCIENCE OF THE UNIVERSITY OF CHICAGO
IN CANDIDACY FOR THE DEGREE OF
DOCTOR OF PHILOSOPHY

BY

WILMER CAVE FRANCE

Printed by
SPOTTISWOODE & CO., NEW-STREET SQUARE, LONDON
1896

CONTENTS

CHAPTER I

JULIAN AND THE NEW SOPHISTIC 1

CHAPTER II

JULIAN'S RELATION TO PHILOSOPHY 38

CHAPTER III

JULIAN'S STYLE AND VOCABULARY 67

APPENDIX I

THE LETTERS 93

APPENDIX II

JULIAN AND DIO 101

PREFACE

THE CHIEF AIM of the following studies has been, as the title indicates, to give a more complete presentation of Julian's relation to the Rhetoric and Philosophy of the fourth Christian century than has hitherto been attempted. Beyond the brief notices given in histories of literature and philosophy, I know of no other systematic treatment of Julian's relation to the New Sophistic, and there seems to have been no previous discussion of his style.

Whatever interest the fragments *contra Christianos* possess for the student of divinity, they have little significance for the student of literature, and have not been taken into consideration here. Special ackowledgements to books consulted have been made in the proper places; I have reserved for this place the acknowledgement of my general indebtedness to Zeller's *History of Philosophy*, to the monograph of M. Naville, *Julien l'Apostat et sa philosophie du Paganisme*, to Boissier's *La fin du Paganisme*, and to Vacherot's *Ecole d'Alexandrie*.

Of those under whose direction my studies have been pursued I wish to express my thanks to Professor E. A. Sonnenschein of the Mason Science College, to Professor J. P. Postgate of Trinity College, Cambridge, to Professor H. W. Smyth of Bryn Mawr College, to Professor W. G. Hale of the University of Chicago, and, especially, to Professor Paul Shorey of the University of Chicago, who suggested the topic of this dissertation and to whose counsel and criticism I am greatly indebted.

WILMER CAVE FRANCE.

UNIVERSITY OF CHICAGO.

CHAPTER I

JULIAN AND THE NEW SOPHISTIC

AMONG the writers who rank as the classics of the fourth Christian century the Emperor Julian holds the first place. His peculiar position as leader of the revival which was the last systematic effort of the Hellenists to rescue Greek culture from the indifference of Christianity is enough of itself to secure for his works an attention which a mere writer of panegyrics could not arouse. The Sophists Libanius, Themistius, and Himerius owe their importance to the fact that their Letters and Orations help the student to reconstruct the surroundings and influences that worked on Julian. But apart from their interest for the historian of Hellenism, Julian's writings hold a definite place in the history of the development of Greek prose. To show what that place is, and what is Julian's relation to the literary movement of the fourth century, a brief retrospect will be necessary.

The fall of Athens took from the Greeks the independence and the stirring political life that had inspired their orators and historians. For the next century and a half Greek literature, like Greece herself, has no history. Not that there was any cessation of literary activity, but it was exercised in narrow fields, and the philosophers, historians, grammarians, and polyhistors, who are the links between the earlier intellectual life of Greece and its revival under the Greco-Roman Empire, have little significance for the history of Greek prose. Yet they serve to show how rapid was its decay. For philosophical prose, the first sign of that decay had been Aristotle's indifference to style—an indifference that, with Epicurus, turned to something like hostility.[1]

The decline of oratory was no less sudden. Early in the third century B.C. Hegesias of Magnesia stands for the degradation of oratorical prose, and the overthrow of the Demosthenic tradition of a periodic and rhythmical style.[2]

It is significant of the causes of the general feebleness, that the first noteworthy name is that of an historian, and still more significant of the source of the coming revival is the fact that Polybius went to Roman history for a theme. To the student of Greek literature Polybius is mainly interesting as personi-

[1] See Spengel, *Ueber das Studium der Rhetorik bei den Alten*, München, 1842, p. 3.

[2] Of the writings of Hegesias we possess only the few fragments preserved in the quotations of his critics; but subsequent writers on Rhetoric are unanimous in condemnation of his jerky style; his effort to imitate Lysias appears to have been a complete failure. Strabo, xiv. p. 648 : ὁ ῥήτωρ ὃς ἦρξε μάλιστα τοῦ 'Ασιανοῦ λεγομένου παραφθείρας τὸ καθεστηκὸς ἔθος τὸ 'Αττικόν. Cic. *Orator*, § 226 : quam perverse fugiens Hegesias, dum ille quoque imitari Lysiam volt . . . saltat incidens particulas. For a parody of Hegesias' style, Cic. *ad Att.* xii. 6, 1, and for a criticism of it, Dion. Hal. *De Comp.* p. 122 ; and *ibid.* 30, where, speaking of the neglect of τὸ συντιθέναι, he says, οὐδεὶς ᾤετο δεῖν ἀναγκαῖον αὐτὸ εἶναι οὐδὲ συμβάλλεσθαί τι τῷ κάλλει τῶν λόγων. Φύλαρχον λέγω καὶ 'Ηγησίαν τὸν Μάγνητα.

fying the relations between Greece and Rome which make the year 146 B.C. a memorable date. He was one of the first of the Greeks to come into contact with the political life of Rome, and he lived before the frankly expressed admiration of the Romans, and their emulation of Greek literature, had begun to arouse in the degenerate Greeks a feeling of superiority on the score of their past.[1] But while his freedom from this affectation, and his appreciation of the Roman genius, distinguish Polybius, he illustrates, on another side, the lowest level of Greek historical prose, judged by the Attic standard of vocabulary and style. He wrote the Κοινή, as might be expected of a Megalopolitan who had had no Attic training in Rhetoric, and had lived but little in Greece. It was because of this neglect of Attic models that his inartistic and unequal prose found so little favour with Dionysius of Halicarnassus.[2]

The century between Polybius and Dionysius saw the development of all that was best in Latin literature, but for Greek prose it is as blank of distinguished names as the period preceding Polybius. Nevertheless in oratory, at any rate, things had not been standing still. Even when Polybius was writing in the Κοινή, schools of Rhetoric were flourishing at Athens. It is probable that Asianism then still held the field, but early in the second century before Christ

---

[1] Hence his popularity with the Romans. Cic. *De Rep.* ii. 14: Polybium nostrum quo nemo fuit in exquirendis temporibus diligentior.

[2] Dion. Hal. *De Comp.* 4. That Dionysius did not hesitate to go to Polybius for his subject-matter, Kaibel has shown in *Hermes* 20: 'Dionysius v. Halikarnassus.'

its supremacy was challenged, and its waning popularity is marked by the appearance, about this time, of the Τέχνη of Hermagoras of Temnos. Hermagoras, by inaugurating a reaction in favour of scientific Rhetoric, paved the way for scientific Atticism and a school of style.[1] Yet he did not set up an ideal of the regeneration of Greek oratory through Atticism, such as later inspired Dionysius. The importance of Hermagoras lies in the fact that he made the first effort, since Aristotle and Theophrastus, to give to Rhetoric a distinct system and function, and so to raise it to the dignity of a science, and that in advising the study of ancient models, he drew attention to style as well as to subject-matter.[2]

The history of Greek prose in the last half-century of the Roman Republic is the history of the development of two schools of oratory, the Attic and the Asianic.[3] The direct or Greek evidences of that development we are not permitted to see. It is from Latin writers that we must judge of the character of Asianism and Atticism at this period. Cicero wrote of them from the point of view of a Roman orator, and Quintilian as a critic of Roman oratory, and a discussion of

[1] The Asianic orators were usually men of little rhetorical training. Dion. Hal. *De Comp.* p. 206 : ἄνθρωποι τῆς μὲν ἐγκυκλίου παιδείας ἄπειροι, τὸ δ' ἀγοραῖον τῆς ῥητορικῆς μέρος ὁδοῦ τε καὶ τέχνης χωρὶς ἐπιτηδεύοντες. Cf. Blass, *Griech. Bered.* p. 56.

[2] On Hermagoras, see Volkmann, *Rhetorik*, p. 5. Blass, *Griech. Bered. von A. bis A.* pp. 84-8. Jebb, *Attic Orators*, ii. 444-5. Wilkins, Introduction to Cic. *De Oratore*, p. 44, and *Hermagoras*, von Georg Thiele, Strassburg, 1893.

[3] The words Attic and Asianic, as has been frequently pointed out, should be taken to denote a difference of ideal, and have little geographical significance; the Atticists themselves came chiefly from Asia.

Attic and Asianic rhetoric here becomes, necessarily, a discussion of the attitude of Cicero and his contemporaries to these opposing tendencies, such as would be out of place in these introductory remarks.[1] It is enough to note that the Roman schools of oratory, of which Hortensius, the follower of the Asianic school, and the Atticist, Calvus, are the typical representatives, must have had their counterparts in the schools of Greece and Asia Minor. It was at Rome, the literary centre of the world, that the struggle between them was carried on; and of the influence exercised on Greek oratory by Roman, at this time, we can judge from the Greek critic, Dionysius of Halicarnassus. His importance for the study of the classic period of Greek literature and of the literature of the revival can hardly be over-estimated. In the early years of the Roman Empire he wrote, at Rome, an appreciation of the Greek prose masterpieces, which has formed the basis of all subsequent criticism. But, though none can have realised more clearly than did Dionysius, that the Golden Age of Greek literature could never return, because the conditions by which it had been inspired could never be renewed, he was far from contenting himself with the contemplation of a glorious past. His hopes for the future of Greek prose, and his high ideal of what that prose must be, connect Dionysius closely with the literary activity of the whole Greco-Roman period. He imagined, with the author of the περὶ ὕψους,[2] that a sincere and

---

[1] See Blass, *Griech. Bered. von A. bis A.* pp. 104 sqq.

[2] *Auct.* περὶ ὕψους, xiii. : καὶ τούτου γε ἀπρὶξ ἐχώμεθα τοῦ σκοποῦ (i.e. τῆς τῶν ἔμπροσθεν μεγάλων συγγραφέων καὶ ποιητῶν μιμήσεώς

sedulous imitation of the Greek masterpieces might lead to the development of a Greek prose which should have something of the spirit as well as the form of its models. Like Polybius, Dionysius was unfettered by the later conventional literary attitude towards the Romans. It was the improvement in Greek oratory which led him to hope for a revival of Greek prose, and that improvement, as he frankly admits, was due to Rome.[1] So rapid had been the change, that Dionysius expressed the hope that the next generation might see the last of that θεατρικὴ καὶ ἀνάγωγος ῥητορική.[2] The question how far his ideals of Greek prose were realised by the writers who came after him is one of the most interesting in the history of the later Greek literature, but it can hardly be more than suggested here. That he exercised any direct influence on subsequent Greek prose seems improbable, for he is hardly mentioned except by Quintilian.[3]

The first century of the Roman Empire is a transition period in Greek literature. Dionysius, writing under Augustus, recognised that the revival, of which he thought he saw the beginning, must

τε καὶ ζηλώσεως). πολλοὶ γὰρ ἀλλοτρίῳ θεοφοροῦνται πνεύματι τὸν αὐτὸν τρόπον ὃν καὶ ἡ Πυθία, κ.τ.λ. Dion. Hal. *Vett. Scriptt. Censura*, i.: ἡ γὰρ ψυχὴ τοῦ ἀναγινώσκοντος ὑπὸ τῆς συνεχοῦς παρατηρήσεως τὴν ὁμοιότητα τοῦ χαρακτῆρος ἐφέλκεται.

[1] Dion. Hal. *De Orr. Antt.* 3 : αἰτία δ' οἶμαι καὶ ἀρχὴ τῆς τοσαύτης μεταβολῆς ἐγένετο ἡ πάντων κρατοῦσα Ῥώμη, πρὸς ἑαυτὴν ἀναγκάζουσα τὰς ὅλας πόλεις ἀποβλέπειν. Cf. Quint. x. 5, 17.

[2] Dion. Hal. *loc. cit.*

[3] Rohde, *Rhein. Mus.* 41, finds no trace of the influence of Dionysius. Hermogenes mentions him only in passing (*de Id.* p. 342, 10, Spengel). Cf. however Anon. apud Spengel, *R. G.* i. 460: Διονύσιος ὃν κανόνα ἄν τις εἴποι δικαίως τῆς περὶ ῥητορικὴν μελέτης.

depend on Roman patronage and encouragement. Under the Emperors who followed Augustus such a revival had little chance of success. But, with the more propitious times, the *rara temporum felicitas* that dawned with Nerva and Trajan, we meet the first representatives of a line of Greek prose writers which continues, with hardly a break, into the last years of the Roman Empire.

In Plutarch and Dio Chrysostom the ideal of Dionysius is more nearly realised than in any late Greek writer, except Lucian. Plutarch, by reason of his Platonic studies, and Dio through his connection with the Sophists, illustrate the beginnings of the two movements that are the final intellectual achievements of Hellenism. Plutarch's interests were devoted to philosophy and history, and, as his concern was with the subject-matter rather than the form, he seems to have had little to do with rhetoric, though he was in friendly relations with the Sophists of his day.[1]

Dio, on the other hand, was, for a part of his life at any rate, a professed Sophist, and he is ranked by Philostratus among the followers of the New Sophistic. He is, however, free from certain of its faults. The fashion of imitating a special author, which had begun as early as Hegesias, became general later, with the complete development of the New Sophistic under Hadrian and the Antonines.[2] Dio, like Plutarch,

[1] For Plutarch's relation to Sophistic, see Volkmann, *Plutarch*, i. 67.

[2] *E.g.* Aristides copied Demosthenes; Herodes Atticus, Critias; Libanius, Aristides; while Arrian so little understood the rules for imitation laid down by Dionysius, that he mixed his styles, now writing Thucydidean, now Herodotean or Xenophontic Greek. Cf. *Hermes*, xx. p. 508 (Kaibel) and Schmid, *Atticismus*, ii. p. 9.

is free from this pedantry, and his easy flowing style was rightly appreciated by his contemporaries. To say of a man that he wrote 'better than Dio' was high praise.[1] The Greek of both Plutarch and Dio reflects a wide reading and close study of authors of the classical period, and is far removed from the Κοινή. But it has nothing of the frigid correctness of Aristides, and its Atticism is comparatively unconscious.[2]

What is true of Plutarch and Dio is true, in a higher degree, of Lucian. Like Dio, he followed, for a time, the profession of a Sophist, and deserted it for the less showy studies of philosophy and literature. In Lucian we see the happiest result of a rigorous training in the schools of Rhetoric, in the case of a man whose original genius kept him free from pedantic imitation of vocabulary and style. But such an apparition is unique in the later history of Greco-Roman literature. The representative writers of his period and of the two following centuries are, with hardly an exception, closely identified with the New Sophistic.[3]

[1] οὗτος ὁ ἄνθρωπος Δίωνος πολὺ κάλλιον γράφει, Epictetus, iii. 23, 17.

[2] For Plutarch's opinion of hyper-Atticism, which meant, in most cases, the unskilful sprinkling in of archaic or farfetched Attic words (ridiculed in Lucian's *Lexiphanes*), see Plutarch, *de Audiendo*. For the fourth century, cf. Themistius, 253, CD.

[3] The term New Sophistic is used, as Philostratus used it, to denote the oratorical revival of the later Greco-Roman period. For while there had been no break in rhetorical studies (as Strabo's account of the Greek rhetoricians, Seneca's descriptions of the schools, and Pliny's reference to Isaeus would prove), the non-forensic style of oratory became more and more prominent in the reigns of the Hellenising Emperors from Nerva to Commodus; and we can only begin to judge of it from Dio Chrysostom.

Every historian of the Greco-Roman period has been at pains to point out the weaknesses of these rhetoricians, who, at any rate for the period between Plutarch and Plotinus, represented all the interests, rhetorical, philosophical, and historical, of the literature of Rome, Greece, and Asia Minor. Their ideal was, it is true, in most cases no higher than the satisfaction of the degenerate tastes of their audiences.[1] An orator of the New Sophistic must improvise, to be successful, and could count on delighting his hearers with a sing-song refrain, and feats of memory or of pantomimicry. If Dionysius could have been present at one of the theatrical $ἐπιδείξεις$ of Polemo or Scopelian or Herodes Atticus, he would probably have found in them all those glaring faults, all that $ἀναίδεια$ $θεατρική$, which he had so severely criticised, and which he had thought was giving place to a more correct and sober standard. He would have found them, moreover, flourishing under the patronage of those very Romans from whose severer taste he had hoped so much. But that was the public or epideictic side of the New Sophistic. If he had turned to the schools of Rhetoric in which those men were trained, and over which they presided, the schools for which those displays of eloquence were, in most cases, an advertisement, he would have found a system of Greek education which might have satisfied him in its methods, however little he would have approved of its results. He would have found a diligent study of classic models too often carried on in a spirit of narrow pedantry, and an ideal of Atticism in vocabulary, far removed from his broader conception of a revived

---

[1] $τὴν τέχνην ὁρίζεσθαι τῷ χαρίζεσθαι$, Aristid. Or. 50, p. 566 D.

national Greek prose.¹ Of the extent to which Atticism in vocabulary was carried in the actual declamations of the Sophists, we can hardly form a judgment from the fragments preserved by Philostratus. The slight remains of Herodes Atticus and of Polemo that we possess are orations which were probably carefully worked over for publication, and the improvisations of these Sophists may have been in a very different style.² But it was under the wing of Sophistic that Atticism, both of vocabulary and style, flourished, and if Aristides must be regarded as exceptional, because he did not improvise, yet his orations show what could be achieved by a scientific study of classic authors, such as the schools of Rhetoric must have encouraged.³ For in Aristides we have the phenomenon of a Mysian of the second Christian

---

¹ Dionysius Hal. (cf. *ad Pomp.* 2. 3) is distinguished from the later theoretical rhetoricians by his use of ἑλληνίζειν, rather than ἀττικίζειν.

² Phrynichus (Lobeck, p. 271) proves that Polemo employed a grammarian to correct some of his published writings, and this may have been the case with the extant declamations. Cf. Rohde, *Rhein. Mus.* xli. p. 185 n.

³ Historians who (like Blass, *op. cit.* p. 89, and Rohde, *Rhein. Mus.* xli.) see in the Sophistic Ἐπίδειξις a direct descent from Asianism, as represented by Hegesias and Hortensius, must admit that, while in their effort to satisfy the Greek love of improvisation, men like Polemo and Herodes Atticus were betrayed into precisely that dithyrambic abuse of bold metaphors, and those hyperbolic expressions, which are associated with the florid Asianic style, yet it would not be fair to condemn them along with Hegesias, who thought himself superior to Demosthenes. The fact seems to be that absolute distinctions cannot here be maintained, for it is certain that an effort after pure Attic speech and careful studies in style were made in the schools of the second Christian century by Sophists whom Rohde condemns for reviving Asianism.

century writing Demosthenic Greek.[1] In the absence of worthy themes in contemporary life Aristides was thrown back on the themes of the schools, and the inevitable result is an effect of artificiality and pedantry. Aristides was proverbially unpopular as a teacher of Rhetoric, probably because of his lack of the talent for improvisation,[2] though for the later Sophists he ranked with Demosthenes himself as a model of Greek prose (Themistius, 330 c).

But in inferior writers the linguistic revival only increased that $\dot{a}\pi\epsilon\iota\rho o\kappa a\lambda\iota a$ in the use of archaisms, to produce astounding effects, which had irritated Dionysius, Plutarch, and Lucian, and which, in the middle of the third century, meets us in the anecdotes of Athenaeus.[3] And side by side with the honest, if mistaken, efforts of Aristides, there must have been a good deal of wholesale plagiarism.[4]

After that period of literary activity under the Antonines, of which Aristides is, for us, the most important representative, there comes another break

---

[1] Aristides' conception of Atticism would have been too narrow for Dionysius. Cf. Aristid. *Rhet.* ii. 6: περὶ δὲ ἑρμηνείας τοσοῦτον ἂν εἴποιμι, μήτε ὀνόματι μήτε ῥήματι χρῆσθαι ἄλλοις πλὴν τοῖς ἐκ τῶν βιβλίων. His practice, however, lagged behind his theory, as may be seen from Schmid's list of his innovations, *Atticismus*, vol. ii. p. 225.

[2] The comment of Philostratus on Aelian's choice of a profession shows that the mere writer held a much less distinguished position than a declaimer. προσρηθεὶς σοφιστὴς ... οὐδὲ ἐπήρθη ὑπὸ τοῦ ὀνόματος οὕτω μεγάλου ὄντος, ἀλλ' ἑαυτὸν εὖ διασκεψάμενος ὡς μελέτῃ οὐκ ἐπιτήδειον τῷ ξυγγράφειν ἐπέθετο, *V. S.* 273. 624.

[3] Plut. *De Aud.* 7. 9, Lucian, *Bis Acc.* 26, and *Lexiphanes* Athenaeus, Speech of Cynulcus at the banquet.

[4] *E.g.* Lucian, *Jup. Trag.* 14, which is probably intended to ridicule this tendency; and cf. D. H. *Lys.* 17.

in the line of noteworthy Greek prose writers, which it may not be fanciful to connect with the unsettled state of the Roman Empire, and the consequent withdrawal of imperial patronage, which lasted from the death of Marcus Aurelius to the reign of Alexander Severus. *Et spes et ratio studiorum in Caesare tantum* is true for the whole period of the Greco-Roman Empire, as for Juvenal's day. The decadence which set in with Commodus lasted through the third century, in which Aelian and Philostratus are the only important representatives of Greek prose. Philostratus wrote his superficial 'Lives' in florid Greek full of reminiscences and hackneyed allusions, and without any pretence to a periodic style or a pure Attic vocabulary.

Aelian hardly deserves to rank as a writer of Greek prose. Perhaps nothing shows more plainly the worthlessness of Philostratus's criticisms, for style and vocabulary, at any rate, than his estimate of the Greek of Aelian. He declares that, though Aelian was a Roman, ἠττίκιζε ὥσπερ οἱ ἐν τῇ μεσογείᾳ Ἀθηναῖοι. He can have had a very superficial notion of what Atticism really was. Aelian wrote a mixture of Homeric, Tragic, and Ionic Greek, or rather patched his Κοινή[1] with it, though he professed to write for πεπαιδευμένα ὦτα.[2]

The half-century between Severus and Constantine furnishes practically no material for the study of revived Greek prose, for the philosophic writings of Plotinus and Porphyry can hardly be associated with the literary efforts of the Sophists. Philostratus had brought his 'Lives' down to the reign of Severus.

---

[1] Schmid, *Att.* vol. iii.   [2] Aelian, *V. H.* 14. 47.

Eunapius, when in the latter half of the fourth century he took up the thread of biography, ignored the third century Sophists. The schools of Rhetoric must have continued to flourish, but favourable outward conditions and imperial patronage were needed to produce another period of activity such as that under the Antonines. Such conditions, however, as had encouraged the earlier renaissance could hardly recur. The way for it had been paved by a series of Hellenising emperors. The impetus which Nero had given to Hellenism had never lost its force and was at its strongest in the second century. In the sphere of Philosophy there was, as yet, no dominant school to rival the claims of Rhetoric, and its literary interests were closely allied with the official archaic religion which it was the policy of the Antonines to support. The second century Sophists had the emperor in their audience, and, for their theatre, Rome and Athens. There is a brilliance, a dignity, and a charm of romance about a career like that of Polemo or Herodes Atticus, which the superficial anecdotes of Philostratus and the dull gossip of Aulus Gellius cannot obscure.

Under the house of Constantine the New Sophistic had a far less brilliant phase. The seat of empire was now Constantinople, which could not furnish the appreciative audiences of the older capital, audiences such as had listened to Herodes and Fronto[1] in the

[1] For the popularity of Greek ἐπιδείξεις at Rome, even with those who did not understand Greek, see Philostr. V. S. 2. 10. 8, and 1. 9. 7. A long contact with Greece and Greek form had made the Romans apt critics of the dramatic changes of expression, the musical voice, the εὔροια, all that made up the Periclean charm that

days when the Roman chair of Rhetoric, ὁ ἄνω θρόνος, was the crowning distinction of a Sophist's career. And the imperial patronage had been transferred to the Christian Church, never again to be given so unreservedly to Rhetoric, except, for a few ineffectual months, by the Emperor Julian.[1]

In the field of Hellenism the third century had produced a formidable rival. When we turn from the 'Lives' of Philostratus to those of Eunapius it seems at first sight as though Sophistic had been thrust into the background by this new interest—the Neoplatonic philosophy. For Eunapius, though he was himself a Sophist, and had the most superficial acquaintance with the doctrines of the school of philosophy that was most prominent in his day, devotes the greater part of his work to the followers of Plotinus and Iamblichus, and treats of the Sophists in a digression.[2] His sketch of Libanius is short and superficial; he disposes of Himerius in a few lines, and omits Themistius altogether. This deficiency is made good by the Orations of Themistius and Himerius and the Orations and Letters of Libanius and of the Emperor Julian. It is from them that we must reconstruct the character and judge of the importance of Rhetoric in the fourth Christian century.

sat on the lips of every Sophist, if we may believe Philostratus. For the prismatic brilliance of the second century declaimer, see Philostr. V. S. 226. 528 K.

[1] Constantius never invited a Sophist or a philosopher to court. ἐκτείνων τὴν ἀπὸ τῶν ἱερῶν ἐπὶ τὴν τῶν λόγων ἀτιμίαν· εἰκότως. ... συγγενῆ γὰρ ταῦτα ἀμφότερα, ἱερὰ καὶ λόγοι κ.τ.λ. Libanius, iii. p. 437 R. Offices were held by low-born Christians, οἱ δὲ ῥήτορες εἱστήκησάν τε καὶ ἔτρεμον, ibid. p. 452.

[2] Eunap. Vit. 107: ἐπανιτέον δὲ ἐπὶ τοὺς φιλοσόφους πάλιν, ὅθεν ἐξέβημεν.

We find, in the first place, very little evidence of a displacement of Sophistic by Philosophy, such as the partiality of Eunapius and the popularity of the Neoplatonic school might have led us to expect.[1] The fourth century Sophists lack the distinction and the interest of their prototypes of the second century because they were allowed less brilliant opportunities. But we do not find that their rivals, the philosophers, fared any better. At the court of Constantine and Constantius Pagan philosophy and Pagan rhetoric were equally under a cloud.

With the changed position of the Sophists the actual scene of their rhetorical triumphs had changed, when the centre of gravity of Roman conquest and government had shifted to the East. The Hellenisation of the East, begun by Alexander, had taken a fresh start when Nero, by openly recognising the supremacy of Greek culture, led the reaction against purely Western interests. Under his successors numerous schools of Rhetoric were founded in remote regions which had formerly been regarded by the Greeks as hopelessly barbarian. To these schools, as the outposts of Hellenism, we can trace that widespread knowledge of Greek letters which we find in the Egypt and Asia Minor of the fourth Christian century.[2]

[1] In the use of the term 'Sophist,' the distinction recognised by Eunapius is preserved, *i.e.* it is confined to rhetoricians who, like Libanius, taught rhetoric and gave ἐπιδείξεις. It may be noted, however, that many Neoplatonic philosophers were renowned for eloquence. So Porphyry chose philosophy, εἰς ἄκρον ἁπάσης ἀφικόμενος καὶ ῥητορικῆς· πλὴν ὅσον οὐκ ἐπ' ἐκείνην ἔνευσε, φιλοσοφίας γε πᾶν εἶδος ἐκματτόμενος, Eunap. p. 456 (Didot).

[2] It is noteworthy that, in the centuries which elapsed between

Nicomedia, Antioch, Smyrna, and Caesarea had become the rivals of Athens, Alexandria, and Constantinople. Libanius of Antioch could boast that his school had supplied with rhetoricians 'three continents and all the islands as far as the Pillars of Heracles.'[1] These large cities, no less than the smaller towns, appreciated the value for their reputation and general prosperity of the presence of a celebrated Sophist,[2] and there was keen rivalry among them to secure for their chairs of Rhetoric a Libanius or a Themistius.[3]

With the philosophers, whom they far outnumbered,[4] these professors of epideictic oratory had

Hyperides and Themistius, not a single Hellene, in the strict sense of the word, with the exception of Polybius and Plutarch, gained distinction in philosophy or literature. With these exceptions, the names which stand out as the classics of the Greco-Roman period belong to the natives of Asia Minor, Syria, and Egypt. Themistius, himself a Paphlagonian, studied rhetoric in Colchis near Phasis. οὐδὲ ἐν ἡμέρῳ χωρίῳ καὶ ῞Ελληνι, ἀλλ' ἐν τῇ ἐσχατιᾷ τοῦ Πόντου, πλησίον Φάσιδος ... οὕτω βάρβαρον καὶ ἀνήμερον χωρίον ἀνδρὸς ἑνὸς σοφία ῾Ελληνικόν τε ἐποίησε καὶ ἀνάκτορον τῶν Μουσῶν, ὃς ἐν μέσῳ Κόλχων καθιδρύμενος, ἐδίδασκε ῥητορικὴν ἐκπονεῖν καὶ πανηγύρεσιν ῾Ελλήνων ἐμπρέπειν, Them. 333 A.

[1] Or. 29, p. 444 R.

[2] Libanius (Or. 29, p. 220) warned the people of Antioch that Caesarea had already robbed them of one Sophist by the offer of a higher salary, and bade them not neglect rhetoric, the cause of their greatness; cf. Philostr. Vit. Scop. 21, 4. The people of Clazomenae begged Scopelian to settle there: προβήσεσθαι τὰς Κλαζομενὰς ἐπὶ μέγα ἡγουμένων εἰ τυιοῦτος ἀνὴρ ἐμπαιδεύσοι σφίσιν.

[3] On the occasion of his visit to Rome, the Romans tried to secure Themistius for their chair of rhetoric, but he would not leave Constantinople. ... αὐτὸς δὲ ὀπίσω παρ' ὑμᾶς, ἱέμην χεῖράς τε ἐπειρῶντο προσάγειν καὶ ἐπίκουρον τῷ ἔρωτι τὸν μέγαν παρακαλεῖν βασιλέα, Them. 298 D.

[4] Themist. 341: ἅτε οὖν οὕτω δεξιοὺς ὄντας, καὶ χειροήθεις, καὶ οἱ

little in common. The old quarrel between Rhetoric and Philosophy had lasted through eight centuries, and was to last to the end. Their mutual jealousies made it as difficult in the fourth century as it had been in the second to be at once a philosopher and a Sophist. Facility in speaking, εὐγλωττία, was still regarded with suspicion,[1] and a single appearance on a platform[2] was enough to disqualify a man for the exclusive ranks of the philosophers, whose attitude to the over-clever Sophists, with their flow of fine language and indifference to speculation, was that of professional men to quacks.[3] Most Sophists were content to know just enough philosophy to enable them to point out the futility of the remainder, and to take their stand with Aristides,[4] who, in this respect at any rate, is representative of his class.

In the second century the rhetoricians of the better sort had ended by deserting from rhetoric to

ἄνθρωποι ἀντασπάζονται (τοὺς σοφιστὰς) καὶ ἀντεπαινοῦσι, καὶ ἐντεῦθεν πλείη μὲν γαῖα τούτων πλείη δὲ θάλασσα· οἱ δὲ ἀπὸ τῆς Σωκράτου γενεᾶς εἰκότως ἄρα καὶ ἐν δίκῃ ἀπεφθίκασί τε καὶ ἀπερρυήκασιν ἐν τῷ παρόντι. Cf. Julian 78 c: παρέσχεσθε γὰρ ὑμεῖς τῶν ἀνδρῶν τούτων ἀφθονίαν, ἀσμένως ἐπακούοντες.

[1] So, in the second century, Φαβωρῖνον τὸν φιλόσοφον ἡ εὐγλωττία ἐν σοφισταῖς ἐκήρυττεν, Philostr. V. S. i. 8, cf. ibid. Proœm. 7, and i. 6; Vit. Apollon. v. 40: ἡ δὲ τοῦ Δίωνος φιλοσοφία ῥητορικωτέρα τῷ 'Α. ἐφαίνετο κ.τ.λ.; and Lucian, Parasit. 2.

[2] Themist. 243 A.

[3] Themistius often defends himself from the stock charge of over-cleverness brought against οἱ δαιμόνιοι σοφισταί, 310 c, 332, 336, 339.

[4] For his scorn of philosophic speculation, see Or. 46. 253 D. This was turning the tables on the Epicureans, who only concerned themselves with rhetoric that they might demonstrate its worthlessness. Cf. Dion. Hal. de Comp. p. 188: 'Επικουρείων δὲ χόρον οἷς οὐδὲν μέλει τούτων, παραιτούμεθα. τὸ γὰρ ' οὐκ ἐπιπόνου τοῦ γράφειν ὄντος,' ὡς αὐτὸς 'Επικούρειος λέγει ' τοῖς μὴ στοχαζομένοις τοῦ πυκνὰ μεταπίπτοντος κριτηρίου ' πολλῆς ἀργίας ἦν καὶ σκαιότητος ἀλεξιφάρμακον.

C

philosophy,[1] like Lucian and Dio. Themistius, whose love of display was always laying siege to his philosophic aspirations, would not admit that they were incapable of reconciliation.[2] Technically, he was a Sophist; that is to say, he gave ἐπιδείξεις, wrote exercises after the Sophistic pattern, and went on embassies which were entrusted to him solely on account of his persuasive charm. But he insisted that, by the Platonic definition, he was no Sophist.[3] He grounded his claim on the single fact that he took no fees:[4] an argument that was quite out of date and would have made a philosopher of Aristides himself,[5] and, moreover, missed the essential point of Plato's quarrel with the earlier Sophists and their τέχνη ἄτεχνος, their superficiality, and preference for opinion over knowledge, and their mechanical rules of art, defects which were as conspicuous in the fourth Christian century as in the days of Gorgias.

On the strength of his Aristotelian 'Paraphrases,'[6]

[1] Lucian, *Bis Acc.* and Fronto, p. 150 (to Marcus Aurelius): Tu mihi videre... laboris taedio defessus, eloquentiae studium reliquisse, et ad philosophiam devertisse, ubi nullum prooemium cum cura excolendum, nulla argumenta quaerenda, nihil exaggerandum, &c.

[2] He described them as suffering equally from their estrangement, and his picture of Rhetoric unsupported by Philosophy is as unflattering as Lucian's, from whom he may have borrowed it. Cf. Themist. 304, *Bis Acc.* 31.

[3] 103 B, 429, 354 D.

[4] Themist. *Or.* xxi. xxvi. 260 c, 345 c, *et passim*.

[5] Aristides took no fees, *Or.* xlvi. p. 192. Those who wished to flatter him called him a philosopher, though he disclaimed the title. Cf. *loc. cit.* οὔκουν μέτεστί μοι τοῦ πράγματος οὐδέν with *Or.* xxvi. 507, 576.

[6] Yet he never uses them to support his claim to the title of Philosopher, and, in the only passage where he refers to them (*Or.* 23. 294–5), he blames the indiscretion of friends who had

Themistius had, perhaps, more right than any one of his century to assert himself against the public which was neither content that a Sophist should speak nor that a philosopher should be silent.[1] But when we consider his wish to reconcile Philosophy and Rhetoric, it must be remembered that, if the new Sophistic differed in most of its essential features from the Sophistic of Plato's contemporaries, it was Philosophy as conceived by Isocrates rather than Plato that Themistius had in mind. Like Aristides (*Or.* 46. 408, 518), he would have Philosophy stand for ἡ διατριβὴ περὶ λόγους παιδεία κοινῶs—that is to say, he would have been content with a Rhetoric grounded on ethics, a conception that was not likely to satisfy the mystical, speculative Neoplatonists who represented fourth century Philosophy. He succeeded only in estranging both sides from himself, and had no resource but to appeal to the Socratic precedent; he reminded the philosophers that Plato had taught in public, and called himself a practical philosopher of the same type,[2] a comparison which proves how completely, in common with the rest of his age, he lacked a sense of proportion.[3]

published these notes which he had taken as a youth (probably from his father's lectures, see *Note on Eugenius*, chapter ii. p. 39) and intended for his private use in his Aristotelian studies.

[1] Themist. σιωπῶντα μὲν φιλόσοφον λοιδοροῦντες ὡς δι' ἀδυναμίαν τοῦ λέγειν σεμνότητα σχηματιζόμενον, λέγοντι δὲ ἐπιτιμῶντες ὡς ἐκ φιλοσοφίας εἰς ῥητορικὴν μετιόντι.

[2] Themist. 245 D.

[3] An age when Plotinus was more read than Plato; Eunap. *Vit. Plot.* τὰ βιβλία (Πλωτίνου) οὐ μόνον τοῖς πεπαιδευμένοις διὰ χειρὸς ὑπὲρ τοὺς Πλατωνίκους λόγους, ἀλλὰ καὶ τὸ πολὺ πλῆθος ἐς αὐτὰ κάμπτεται. Libanius copied Aristides rather than Demosthenes: ὑπὲρ τῶν ὀρχηστῶν 475: τὸ γὰρ ἡνίκα ἂν ποιῶ λόγους τῶν ἰχνῶν ἔχεσθαι

Libanius, on the other hand, is entirely unconscious of any need for uneasiness as to his position. He was the Aristides of his age, but without the religious *Schwärmerei* of Aristides, and his talent for ἐπίδειξις encouraged him to a greater variety of composition. But, unlike Aristides, he never jeered at philosophic speculation, and nowhere hints at a desire for the title of philosopher.[1] He thought that of ' Sophist ' more honourable than any that the State could bestow,[2] and the most flattering that he could give to Julian,[3] whose oratorical power he rated high. 'Like the nightingale,' he says, 'I ask only to sing,'[4] and, if elsewhere he calls the Sophists τέττιγες, he means to praise (Lib. *Ep.* 304).

Of all the Hellenists who supported Julian's re-

Ἀριστείδου καὶ πειρᾶσθαι τοὺς ἐμοὺς ἀφομοιοῦν εἰς ὅσον οἱόντε τοῖς ἐκείνου κ.τ.λ. Julian declared that Iamblichus was inferior to Plato only in point of time ; Libanius assured Themistius that he was equal to Demosthenes (*Ep.* 371) ; Metrophanes wrote a treatise περὶ τῶν χαρακτήρων Πλάτωνος, Ξενοφῶντος, Νικοστράτου, Φιλοστράτου. Lucian had found it necessary to warn writers μὴ μιμεῖσθαι τῶν ὀλίγου πρὸ ἡμῶν γενομένων σοφιστῶν τὰ φαυλότατα, Suidas, *Metrophanes*; and the highest praise which Eunapius can give to Himerius is, ὅτι παρὰ τὸν θεῖον Ἀριστείδην ἵσταται, Eunap. *Vit.* p. 494.

[1] Libanius separates himself from the philosophers, *Ep.* 244 to Themistius, τῆς σοφίας ἣν δὴ λειμῶνος ποικιλωτέραν δεικνύων πάλαι κρατεῖς, εἰ μὲν καὶ τοὺς ταὐτό σοι καλουμένους, οὐκ οἶδα. Cf. *Ep.* 1072 : ὑμῖν τοῖς φιλοσόφοις.

[2] Eunap. *Vit. Lib.* p. 496 : τῶν ἀξιωμάτων τὸ μέγιστον οὐκ ἐδέξατο, φήσας τὸν σοφιστὴν εἶναι μείζονα.

[3] *Ep.* 43, Wolf's Century : ἄρχων τ' ἀγαθὸς κρατερός τε σοφιστής. Cf. *Epp.* 1059. 33. Julian matched Hermes, *Or.* 23, p. 55.

[4] *Epp.* 707, 736 *et passim*. *Ep.* 13, Wolf's Century : ἀλλ' ἀρκεῖ μοι τὸ ᾄδειν ὥσπερ τῇ ἀηδόνι (ᾄδειν, it may be noted, was the Sophistic word for an ἐπίδειξις). Cf. Dio Chr. *Or.* 32, p. 423, Julian 105 A, Philostr. *Vit. S. Hadrian.* Aristid. 50, 564, 703.

rival, Libanius of Antioch was the most conservative. A second century purist could have found no falling off from sophistic etiquette either in his point of view or his treatment of his themes. And he was as punctilious as any one of them in his avoidance of Roman names, and, as far as possible, of Roman allusions.[1] This was a tradition which had naturally much weakened in the Byzantine period. Themistius neglects it entirely, Himerius betrays only rarely his sense of the earlier etiquette by using a circumlocution rather than, directly, a Roman name. In a panegyric of Julian it required much ingenuity to avoid mention of the earlier Roman Emperors, especially of Marcus Aurelius, Julian's model. Libanius not only accomplished this, but never used a Latin word or expression, though he lived in a period when Latin was still the official language,[2]

[1] Aristides in his panegyric of Rome used no Roman name, and declared that one of the virtues of the ideal ruler is τὸ φιλέλληνα εἶναι, Or. ix. vol. i. p. 105. Of the innumerable instances of the scrupulous avoidance of these barbarisms in the second century, that recorded of Apollonius of Tyana by Philostratus is one of the most striking. ἀναγνοὺς δὲ καὶ ψήφισμα Ἰωνικὸν ἐν ᾧ ἐδέοντο αὐτοῦ κοινωνῆσαί σφισι τοῦ ξυλλόγου, καὶ ὀνόματι προστυχὼν ἥκιστα Ἰωνικῷ, Λούκουλλος γάρ τις ἐπεγέγραπτο τῇ γνώμῃ, πέμπει ἐπιστολὴν ἐς τὸ κοινὸν αὐτοῦ ἐπίπληξιν ποιούμενος περὶ τοῦ βαρβαρισμοῦ τούτου. καὶ γὰρ δὴ καὶ Φαβρίκιον καὶ τοιούτους ἑτέρους ἐν τοῖς ἐψηφισμένοις εὗρεν, Vit. Ap. 4. 5. Cf. Dio C. Or. 22, p. 505 Rsk. ἴσως δέ μου καταφρονεῖς καὶ ἡγεῖ με ληρεῖν ὅτι οὐ περὶ Κύρου καὶ Ἀλκιβιάδου λέγω ὥσπερ οἱ σοφοὶ ἔτι καὶ νῦν, ἀλλὰ Νέρωνος καὶ τοιούτων πραγμάτων νεωτέρων τε καὶ ἀδόξων μνημονεύω.

[2] Themistius calls Latin ἡ διάλεκτος κρατοῦσα (71 c), but admits that he never acquired it. In fact the best-educated men of the fourth century contented themselves with a knowledge of Greek. Libanius needed an interpreter for a Latin letter (Lib. Ep. 956, 1241). Julian's knowledge of Latin was probably slight; Eutrop.

and wrote in the reign of one Emperor who knew no Greek.[1] He could think of Julian only as a Hellene,[2] a literary man,[3] an orator,[4] a Sophist who condescended to public business,[5] and, when he is writing to a philosopher who had trained Julian, as an expert in philosophy.[6] His influence on Julian began when the latter, shortly after his release from his six years' imprisonment in Cappadocia, was allowed to leave Constantinople to pursue his studies at Nicomedia.[7] There he found Libanius,[8] and, perhaps, Themistius.[9] It was to

---

x. 16 : adeo ut Latina eruditio nequaquam cum Graeca scientia conveniret. This is perhaps nearer the truth than Libanius' praise of Julian's proficiency in both tongues, Liban. i. p. 529. For other instances of the neglect of Latin in the first half of the fourth century cf. Sievers, *Leben Libanius*, p. 13. With the rise of law-schools, and especially of the famous school at Berytus, under the emperors following Julian, Latin came into fashion again, and Libanius lived to complain that it was likely to oust Greek, *Or.* 65, p. 442 R.; *Epp.* 1125, 209, 567, 566, 1062, 1123. Libanius saw with dismay the gradual neglect of Greek literature and the Greek language in favour of the utilitarian study of Latin law and literature, *Orr.* i. 133, 185, ii. 539, 541; *Epp.* 777, 1123.

[1] Valens, Ammianus, xxxi. 14.

[2] Lib. i. p. 458: Ἕλλην τις εἶ καὶ κρατεῖς Ἑλλήνων. Cf. Himerius, *Or.* 7 (of Julian), πάλιν Ἀθῆναι τὰς αὐτῶν ὠδῖνας προσφθέγγονται.

[3] *Ep.* 9, Wolf's Century.

[4] *Ep.* 43, Wolf's Century.

[5] *Epp.* 33, 1059, Larger Wolf.

[6] *Ep.* 866 *ad Priscum*.

[7] Eunap. *Vit. Maxim.*

[8] Lib. *Or.* i. 38–42; *Epp.* 285, 654, 1490. Libanius taught at Nicomedia for five years, 344–9 A.D. For an account of his life there vide Sievers, *Leben*, p. 53.

[9] The evidence for Themistius' sojourn in Nicomedia about this time is not precise. But it is not easy to see how Julian could have been his pupil at any other period. Cf. Julian, *Ep. ad Themist.* 257

his association with Libanius at Nicomedia that Julian owed his Sophistical training, his technical knowledge of epideictic oratory, and to some extent, at any rate, his Greek style. He was under an oath not to attend the Sophist's lectures, but there was no attempt to hinder their daily intercourse, and he diligently studied all that Libanius wrote, so that he ranked as his most apt pupil.[1]

Of Julian's relations with Themistius it is not so easy to speak definitely. He received no appointment at Julian's hands,[2] but neither did Libanius. From Julian himself we gather that he carried on a continuous and friendly correspondence with Libanius, while the long letter to Themistius proves that he had been the latter's pupil,[3] and that Themistius had addressed a letter of exhortation and flattery to him on his accession. Julian deprecates the flattery, and refutes the argument of Themistius in favour of the βίος πρακτικός. In view of the meagre evidence for Julian's attitude to Themistius it would not be

D: λέγοιμ' ἂν ἤδη σοι τὰ τοῦ Πλάτωνος ... εἰδότι μὲν καὶ διδάξαντί με. That Themistius taught at Nicomedia we know from his 24th *Oration*, p. 306. Baret, *De Themistio*, p. 9, assumes too hastily, on the score of the friendship between Libanius and Themistius, that they must have taught at the same time at Nicomedia; they could quite as easily have become acquainted at Constantinople.

[1] Libanius, i. p. 232. It was the Christian sophist Hecebolius, if we may judge from the hints of Libanius, who prevented Julian from attending his lectures.

[2] He held his only prefecture under Theodosius, Them. *Or.* 34, c. xiv. with Mai's note. Baret, p. 22, assumes that it was Julian who offered the prefecture of Constantinople to Themistius, and to whom Themistius refers as ὁ αἰδοῖος ἐμοὶ αὐτοκράτωρ.

[3] Julian, *Ep. ad Them.*

safe to accept the suggestion of some critics that the respectful tone[1] in this letter is ironical.

Libanius in his Orations and Letters has placed his relations with Julian beyond question. But when we turn to the Orations of Themistius we find no trace of such a hero-worship of Julian. Themistius speaks of him with the greatest reserve, and sometimes with an ambiguity which leaves it open to question whether he is referring to Julian or to another emperor. He only once mentions Julian by name,[2] though he alludes to him several times, and always with respect.[3] His indirectness contrasts strongly with the open lamentations of Libanius, expressed at the same period and under the same Christian emperors. But the evidence for actual estrangement is and must remain negative.[4] Themis-

---

[1] Julian, *Ep.* 263: ὦ φιλὴ κεφαλὴ καὶ πάσης ἔμοιγε τιμῆς ἀξία.

[2] ἀρκεῖ βιασθεὶς Ἰουλιανὸς τῆς οἰκουμένης καλέσαι πρεσβευτὴν ἄξιον οὐ μόνον τῆς καλλιπόλεως καὶ τὰ πρῶτα φέρεσθαι φιλοσοφίας ἐν γράμμασιν ὁμολογήσας, Themist. 354 D. This encomium of Themistius' philosophy does not occur in any extant letter of Julian. Lib. *Ep.* 1061 mentions an Oration of Themistius in praise of Julian which is not extant.

[3] Themist. 165 c probably refers to Julian: τῷ παιδὶ τῷ Κωνσταντίνου ἔπειτα τῷ ἐκείνου ἀδελφῷ (*i.e.* cousin) ἀμφοῖν ἀγαθοῖν μὲν καὶ ἀτεχνῶς δίοιν. And perhaps 99 D Themistius is speaking of Procopius, who claimed relationship with Julian, as ὁ τὸν πώγωνα καθειμένος καὶ τοῦ φιλοσοφωτάτου τῶν βασιλέων ἀντιποιούμενος.

[4] Baret, *De Them.* p. 22, and, following him, Zeller, v. p. 742, assume rather too hastily that there was a positive coolness between Julian and Themistius. They agree that the indifference of the latter to the Neoplatonic philosophy (Them. 33 and 295 B) would be sufficient to account for such a coolness. Baret further alleges his Christianismus. If by this he means his high position under the Christian Emperor Constantius, that would certainly be a good reason for Julian's lack of friendliness. Themistius (63 c) thanks

tius seems to have taken no interest in the restoration of Hellenism, and his attitude to Rome and the Romans was very different from that of Libanius.[1] The latter's conviction of the importance of the old national religion for the prosperity of the Roman Empire was one of the strongest ties that bound him to Julian, and they always remained on cordial terms.[2] Libanius declared that the Emperor surpassed his teacher in rhetoric.[3]

Julian's work as a Sophist is, technically speaking, comprised in his panegyrics and his φυσικοὶ ὕμνοι,

---

Jovian for bringing back philosophy from exile: οὐ πάνυ παρὰ τοῖς πολλοῖς εὐπραγοῦσαν κατὰ τὸν παρόντα χρόνον. It would be possible to see in this passage a reflection on Julian's attitude to philosophy in the person of Themistius himself, if it were not more natural to refer it to the alarm felt by the Hellenists on Jovian's accession. Socrates, iii. c. 24 : οἱ τριβωνοφόροι τοὺς τρίβωνας ἀπέθεντο, an alarm which was dispelled by Jovian's declaration of freedom of religious opinion, see Gibbon, vol. ii. 407, Themist. 68 A, 69 D, Dindorf *ad loc.* Baret (p. 27) seems to be wrong in supposing that Themistius' *Oration* (v.) was to advise religious toleration. It was rather to thank Jovian for it ; cf. 68–9.

[1] Themistius' free use of Roman names and allusions has been already noted. He goes so far as to say (71 c) that, if he could do so, he would exchange his knowledge of Greek for a knowledge of Latin that Valens might understand him without an interpreter—a piece of flattery to which so sincere a Hellenist as Libanius would never have condescended.

[2] We find Libanius, even under the Christian Theodosius, vehemently denouncing the desecration of the Pagan temples and tracing the successes and reverses of the Roman emperors to their respect for or neglect of the gods, Lib. *Or.* 28. 179. Libanius was, however, quite free from the taint of superstition, and even declares that he does not hold with sacrifices and haruspices, but prefers ἡ ῥητόρων μαντική, which is τὸ καλῶς εἰκάζειν, *Ep.* 73. 7.

[3] *Ep.* 43, Wolf's Century. The admiration was mutual; see Julian, *Ep.* 14, which praises extravagantly an Oration of Libanius.

but his rhetorical training has left its traces in all his writings, so that we may draw upon them all for illustrations. His first oration, the panegyric of Constantius, is universally acknowledged to be his masterpiece.[1] Julian's study of Rhetoric was comparatively brief and intermittent, and he constantly pleads this fact in order to disarm the criticism of trained rhetoricians.[2] Yet his first Oration follows, with hardly a single deviation, the rhetorical rules for the arrangement and treatment of a βασιλικὸς λόγος as we find them in Menander's treatise on epideictic oratory.

Analysis of Oration I.

It begins with the ἀκροατῶν παρασκευή, the prooemium which conciliates the audience and gives them the threads by which to follow the whole oration.[3] Julian deprecates the charge of flattery,[4] and announces the order of the divisions of his theme.[5]

The formal panegyric begins with ἡ πατρίς.[6]

---

[1] It was on the model of this Oration that Libanius wrote his Oration on Julian's consulship. It was written and probably delivered, c. 355, before Julian went to Gaul.

[2] That this excuse was a commonplace of oratory we may gather from Themistius 332 et passim, Julian, 2 A, D, 3 C.

[3] Menander ap. Spengel 221. 228 insists on such a prooemium for each division of the panegyric; Julian observes this rule by the affectation of ἀπορία (e.g. 6 D); by a question intended to call the attention of the audience to a fresh division, or by a plain statement that he is passing on to it.

[4] 4 C.

[5] 4 D.

[6] 5 B. So Menander, 215: μετὰ τὰ προοίμια ἐπὶ τὴν πατρίδα ἥξεις.

Here comes in the praeteritio which Menander [1] advises in the case of an emperor whose birthplace was not especially renowned, for Constantius was born in Illyria. After an inventory of the nations which can claim a share in the γένεσις καὶ τροφή of Constantius, Julian launches into a brief panegyric of Rome, and awards her the ἐξαίρετον γέρας, as ἡ βασιλεύουσα, as the birthplace of Constantius' mother, and as a city which Constantius had called διδάσκαλον ἀρετῆς.[2] He is able to carry back the προγόνων ἔπαινος[3] as far as Claudius II.,[4] and dwells briefly on the exploits of the ancestors [5] of Constantius, especially of his father Constantine,[6] whose greatest achievement was τὴν σὴν γένεσιν καὶ τροφήν. The mention of filial piety gives a chance for the contrast with the Persian kings without which a βασιλικὸς λόγος would have been incomplete.[7] There were no portents at the birth of Constantius, so Julian 'leaves the recital of them to the poets.' [8] There follows, according to rule,[9] an account

[1] 215 end. Other cases of praeteritio and ἀντίφρασις in Julian are 7 c, 6 c, 7 D, 10 B, &c.
[2] 6 c.
[3] Menander, 217 init.; cf. Julian 105 A: καθάπερ τινὰ ῥήτορα ξὺν τέχνῃ τέλειον ᾆσαι βασιλίδος ἐγκώμιον ἄνωθεν ἀπὸ τοῦ γένους ἀρξάμενον.
[4] Ib. 6 D.
[5] Ib. 7.
[6] Ib. 7-9.
[7] Cf. Themist. 233 A et al. and Dio C. Or. 4 de Regno, for the stock passage from Herodotos.
[8] Julian, 10 B; cf. Menander, 218: εἴ τι σύμβολον γέγονε περὶ τὸν τόκον . . . ἀντεξέτασον τοῖς περὶ τὸν Ῥώμυλον καὶ τὸν Κῦρον, with Julian 10 B: ὅσα ἄλλα θρυλεῖν εἰώθασιν . . . Κύρου καὶ τοῦ τῆς ἡμετέρας οἰκιστοῦ πόλεως (= Ῥωμύλου). Menander says: 'Do not hesitate to invent them,' but Julian will not do this.
[9] Menander, 219, 220.

of Constantius' training in war, letters, and statesmanship, a comparison, to his advantage, with Odysseus and Alcibiades, and next ὁ περὶ τῶν πράξεων λόγος (cf. Menander, 220 end). 'The virtues of a king are four,' says Menander,[1] 'courage, justice, temperance, prudence.' The recital of the wars of Constantius is designed to show his superiority to his contemporaries in all these.

The πράξεων λόγος is naturally the longest. A fresh division begins with the ἕξεις of Constantius, and here there is a second contrast with Alexander and Cyrus. This division, which is technically called ὁ περὶ τῆς εἰρήνης λόγος,[2] is especially concerned with the peaceful virtues of temperance, justice, and prudence,[3] which are illustrated at some length. The happy condition of the Empire and the army under such a ruler is then described, and the pane-

---

[1] Menander, 222; cf. D. C. *de Regno* 26: φιλάνθρωπον ἦθος καὶ πρᾷον καὶ δίκαιον ἔτι δὲ ὑψηλὸν καὶ ἀνδρεῖον καὶ μάλιστα δὴ χαίροντα εὐεργεσίαις ὅπερ ἐστὶν ἐγγυτάτω τῆς τῶν θεῶν φύσεως. Plato had said in the *Laws*, 709 E, τύραννος δ' ἔστω νέος καὶ μνήμων καὶ εὐμαθὴς καὶ ἀνδρεῖος καὶ μεγαλοπρεπὴς φύσει καὶ σώφρων. A βασιλικὸς λόγος was always designed to show that the ruler to whom it was addressed realised Plato's ideal. So Julian, 10 c. Themistius, who lived under Constantius, Julian, Jovian, Valens, Gratian, and Theodosius, and addressed panegyrics to five of these emperors, assures every one of them in turn ὅτι ὅποσα ἐκεῖνος (Plato) ὠνειροπόλησεν ὕπαρ ἡμεῖς τεθεάμεθα, 62 D; cf. 55 (to Constantius), 66 D (to Jovian), 81 A (to Valens), 215 c (to Theodosius).

[2] Menander, 226 *init.*

[3] Cf. Menander, *loc. cit.*: τοῦτον δὲ διαιρήσεις εἰς σωφροσύνην, εἰς δικαιοσύνην, εἰς φρόνησιν. The correspondence with Menander's rules is here especially close. Cf. Julian 46 D, 47 A with Menander 227 *end*, where the illustration of σωφροσύνη is almost verbally the same; and cf. Julian 43 with Menander 230 *init.* Julian says: διὰ τὰς κοινὰς τῶν πόλεων εὐετηρίας; Menander says: ἐρεῖς τὰς εὐετηρίας πόλεων.

gyric ends rather abruptly, without the final εὐχή for the continuance of the happy reign that was recommended by Menander.

The panegyric written by Themistius on Constantius affords in some respects a contrast to Julian's Oration. Themistius too fulfils all the requirements of Menander, but a much closer analysis would be needed to show how skilfully he covers the ground. Julian is so punctilious in following the rules and in indicating the order of his subjects that he leaves the impression that he wrote with a handbook of rhetoric before him.[1] Themistius conceals his art. He is less historical, and devotes himself chiefly to ὁ περὶ τῆς εἰρήνης λόγος. His language throughout is more figurative and picturesque[2] than Julian's, and he occasionally becomes impassioned,[3] while Julian never shows a trace of rhetorical θειασμός.

Julian belonged, with Themistius, to the less conservative class of Sophists, and seldom made an effort to avoid a Roman allusion, but his illustrations were, for the most part, drawn from the classic period of Greece, and while on almost every page of his panegyric there is a mention of Alexander or Cyrus,[4] or both,

---

[1] Yet Julian declines to be bound by the rules of panegyrists, 63 D, 64 A.

[2] Cf. Julian's ὥσπερ ὄφλημα βασιλεῖ πατρῷον ἀποδοὺς τὴν ἁλουργίδα (77 c) with Themistius' (56 B) ἀπεδύσατο οὐ τὸ γῆρας καθάπερ οἱ ὄφεις, ἀλλὰ τὴν ἔξωρον ἁλουργίδα.

[3] On the founding of a library by Constantius, he cries ἰού, ἰού, ὡς ἄτοπον καὶ τεράστιον ἐκεῖνο, ὅτι καὶ τὰς ψυχὰς αὐτὰς τῶν σοφῶν καὶ ἀοιδίμων ἡρώων ἀνακαλεῖται καὶ ἀνίστησιν ἐκ τῶν τάφων, 59 C.

[4] All the Sophists delighted in allusions to Persian monarchs. Lucian ridicules the tendency, Rhet. Pracc. 18 : καὶ ἀεὶ ὁ "Αθως πλείσθω καὶ ὁ Ἑλλήσποντος πεζευέσθω καὶ Ξέρξης φευγέτω.

there is seldom a direct reference to Roman history.[1]
The rest of Julian's purely rhetorical work is comprised in Oration II.[2]—a second panegyric of Constantius—and Oration III., which is a χαριστήριος or *gratiarum actio* addressed to the Empress Eusebia. Both these Orations afford illustrations of many of the points noted in the analysis of Oration I., but do not call for further comment. The second Oration was modelled on the first, of which it is in great part a literal reproduction.[3] The χαριστήριος is important for its autobiographical details.

Julian notes as characteristic of οἱ ἀμαθέστατοι ῥήτορες the habit of introducing at every turn certain hackneyed poetical and mythological allusions. It was a device to hide the meagreness of their subject-matter and their lack of ingenuity in developing their themes.[4] 'They are always quoting Delos, and

[1] τοὺς ἐξελόντας Καρχηδόνα 'Ρωμαίων στρατηγούς; cf. 17 D, 18 A. Once he evidently avoids a Roman name, 10 B: Κύρου καὶ τοῦ τῆς ἡμετέρας οἰκιστοῦ πόλεως (= Romulus) καὶ 'Αλεξάνδρου. To avoid saying Mardonius, Julian uses a circumlocution, 352 A: ὁμώνυμος ἦν τοῦ τὸν Ξέρξην ἀναπείσαντος ἐπὶ τὴν Ἑλλάδα στρατεῦσαι. The highest praise that Julian can give to Rome is that it is 'Ελληνὶς γένος τε καὶ πολιτείαν, 153 A. The avoidance of the direct name in the case of Romulus may have been merely the literary affectation which caused the Sophists to say ὁ λογοποιὸς ὁ Θούριος rather than 'Herodotos' (Julian, 389), and ἡ Λάκαινα rather than 'Helen' (412 D). Julian often does this, though not, like Libanius, to excess.

[2] It was probably never delivered; the date is approximately determined by 56 B, which proves that it was written after Julian's departure to Gaul.

[3] Cf. 57 c with 37 c; 58 B with 38–9; 77 c with 32 A.

[4] 236 A: διὰ τὴν τῶν λόγων ἀπορίαν καὶ τὸ μὴ ἔχειν εὑρεῖν ἐκ τῶν παρόντων ὅ τι φῶσιν.

Leto and her children, and shrill swan-songs and dewy meadows, and the scent of flowers and spring.'[1] Themistius declares that, for his part, he is free from this affectation—καὶ μή με ἄλλως νομίσῃς ὡραΐζεσθαι τῷ κύκνῳ καὶ τῇ ἀηδόνι καθάπερ οἱ κομψοὶ σοφισταί, οἱ κομμοῦντες τοὺς λόγους οἷον φυκίῳ κέχρηνται τούτοις τοῖς ὀρνέοις.[2] Neither Julian nor Themistius uses the trite illustrations mentioned in these passages, though Himerius abounds in them.[3]

But there were many other poetical and literary allusions which had passed into the Sophistic language, and were quite as well-worn as those which Julian avoids. The following tabulation, while it does not pretend to be exhaustive, will show, at any rate, that he followed the Sophistic usage in the matter of these ἡδύσματα λόγων.

---

[1] Julian, 236 A: ἡ Δῆλος ἐπέρχεται καὶ ἡ Λητὼ μετὰ τῶν παίδων, εἶτα κύκνοι λιγυρὸν ᾄδοντες καὶ ἐπηχοῦντα αὐτοῖς τὰ δένδρα λειμῶνές τε ἔνδροσοι καί τινες εἰκόνες τοιαῦται. Ποῦ τοῦτο Ἰσοκράτης ἐν τοῖς ἐγκωμιαστικοῖς ἐποίησε λόγοις; ποῦ δὲ τῶν παλαιῶν τις ἀνδρῶν οἳ ταῖς Μούσαις ἐτελοῦντο γνησίως, ἀλλ' οὐχ ὥσπερ οἱ νῦν.

[2] Themist. 336 c; cf. 330: μινυριζόντων ἐν τοῖς προλόγοις ἦρος ἐπαίνους καὶ χελιδόνων καὶ ἀηδόνων; cf. with this Lucian's description of the degradation of rhetoric, *Bis Acc.* 31: ἐγὼ γὰρ ὁρῶν ταύτην οὐκέτι σωφρονοῦσαν ... κοσμουμένην δὲ καὶ τὰς τρίχας εὐθετίζουσαν καὶ φυκίον ἐντριβομένην ... and D. Hal. *vet. auct. proem*.

[3] Aristides, *Or.* xx. p. 428 D: ὦ κύκνων ᾠδὴ καὶ ἀηδόνων χόρος; Himerius, *Or.* 18. 1 Delos and Leto, *ib.* 4 nightingale and swan; ὀλίγος ὁ λειμὼν τοῦ κύκνου ἀλλ' ᾄδοντι αὐτῷ συνυπηχεῖν ἐθέλει τὰ σύμπαντα; cf. Julian, 236 A: κύκνοι καὶ ἐπηχοῦντα αὐτοῖς τὰ δένδρα; Choricius Gaz. (Boisson) p. 173: οἱ κύκνοι ὑμνοῦσι τὸν Ἀπόλλωνα, cf. Philostr. *Vit. Scop.* 4. Scopelian refused to go to Clazomenae, τὴν ἀηδόνα φήσας ἐν οἰκίσκῳ μὴ ᾄδειν, ὥσπερ δ' ἄλσος τὴν Σμύρναν ἐσκέψατο καὶ τὴν ἠχὼ τὴν ἐκεῖ πλείστου ἀξίαν ᾠήθη. Libanius wrote an ἐγκώμιον ἔαρος, iv. p. 1051, and for the general tendency to this sort of commonplace see Epictetus, iii. p. 282, Teubner.

Herodotos, *Thalia*, 139-140.

Pindar, *Olymp.* vii. 50: κείνοις ὁ μὲν ξανθὰν ἀγαγὼν νεφέλαν | πολὺν ὗσε χρυσόν.

Menander ap. Spengel, 3, p. 362, men-

Julian, 117 B: πυνθάνομαι γὰρ δὴ καὶ Δαρεῖον ἕως ἔτι δορυφόρος ἦν τοῦ Περσῶν μονάρχου, τῷ Σαμίῳ ξένῳ περὶ τὴν Αἴγυπτον συμβαλεῖν φεύγοντι τὴν αὐτοῦ καὶ λαβόντα φοινικίδα τινὰ δῶρον οὗ σφόδρα ἐπεθύμει τὴν Σαμίων ὕστερον ἀντιδοῦναι τυραννίδα, and again in *Ep.* 29.

Themist. 109 A: τὰ μὲν ἄλλα Δαρεῖος ἀφῆκε, Συλοσῶντα δὲ οὐκ ἀφῆκεν. Σάμιος ἦν, καὶ Δαρεῖον στρατευόμενον ἐπειδὴ τῆς χλαμύδος ἁλόντα ᾔσθετο δωρεῖται προῖκα ἐκδύς.

Ib. 67 A: τὸν Ὑστάσπου Δαρεῖον μικρὸν ἀπέφηνας εἰς μεγαλοπρέπειαν ἀμοιβῆς.

Julian 290 B: ἵνα χρυσὸν ὥσπερ τοῖς Ῥοδίοις ὁ Θεὸς ὕσῃ τοῖς πένησιν.

Aristid. i. p. 807: καὶ Ὅμηρος μὲν πλοῦτον ἔφη καταχέαι τὸν Δία τῇ νήσῳ καὶ Πίνδαρος παραλαβὼν ὗσαι χρυσὸν νεφέλην ξανθὴν ἐπιστήσαντα.

Liban. vol. iv. p. 200 R. τοσοῦτον αὐτοῖς ἐν οὐρανῷ

tions as an appropriate ἥδυσμα in a panegyric of Rhodes, περὶ δὲ 'Ροδίων ὅτι ὁ Ζεὺς ὗσεν χρυσῷ.

κεῖσθαι χρυσίον ὥστε καὶ πόλεις ὅλας εὐδαίμονας ποιεῖν ὑετῷ χρυσίου.

Philostr. *Imag.* ii. 27: 'Ροδίοις δὲ λέγεται χρυσὸς ἐξ οὐρανοῦ ῥεῦσαι καὶ διαπλεῦσαι σφῶν τὰς οἰκίας καὶ τοὺς στενωποὺς νεφέλην ἐς αὐτοὺς ῥήξαντος τοῦ Διός, ὅτι κἀκεῖνοι τῆς 'Αθηνᾶς ξυνῆκαν.

Himerius, 13. 34: 'Ροδίους μὲν δὴ λόγος ὑσθῆναι χρυσῷ, χρυσῆν ἐπ' αὐτοὺς τοῦ Διὸς νεφέλην ῥήξαντος.

Choric. Gaz. (Boiss.) 121: ἆρα μὴ τοσοῦτον ἐν πανηγύρει χρυσὸν ἡ 'Ρόδος ἔπεισε μυθολογῆσαι 'Ροδίοις χρυσοῦν ὑετόν.

Homer, *Od.* δ. 227 sqq.

Julian, 240 B: τίς ἡμῖν τὸ νηπενθὲς ἐξεύροι φάρμακον; εἴτε λόγος ἦν ἐκεῖνο πλήρης Αἰγυπτίων διηγημάτων εἴθ' ὅπερ αὐτὸς ἐποίησεν τοῦτο τῆς 'Ελένης παρ' Αἰγυπτίων μαθούσης ... ποταμοὺς εἶναι χρὴ λόγους οἱ τὰς ἀλγηδόνας ἀφαιρήσουσι τῶν ψυχῶν; and again 412 D.

D

Eunap. *Ecl.* 17 : τί ἐν τοῖς ἡμετέροις λόγοις ἐστὶ φάρμακον ὁποῖον "Ομηρος διὰ τοῦ κρατῆρος τοῦ τῆς Ἑλένης αἰνίττεται ... ἢ καὶ τὸ τῆς Ἑλένης φάρμακον οὐ ποά τις ἦν οὐδέ τις Αἰγυπτία τέχνη νηπενθὲς πόμα σκευάζουσα ἀλλά τις λόγος ἡδὺς καὶ πάνσοφος.

Themist. 357 Α : φύεται ἐν τοῖς φιλοσοφίας λειμῶσιν φάρμακον ... ὁποῖον "Ομηρος λέγει τὴν τοῦ Διὸς θυγατέρα Ἑλένην πορίσασθαι παρὰ τῆς Αἰγυπτίας.

Philostr. prooem. to *V. S.* 201 : τὸ φρόντισμα τοῦτο τὰ ἄχθη κουφιεῖ ὥσπερ ὁ κρατὴρ τῆς Ἑλένης τοῖς Αἰγυπτίοις φαρμάκοις.

Eupolis Δημ. 6.

Julian, 33 A : τίς δὲ ἡ πειθὼ τοῖς χείλεσιν ἐπικαθημένη ἢ τὸ κέντρον ἐγκαταλιπεῖν (so Cobet, rightly, for Hertlein's ἐναπολιπεῖν) ἰσχύσασα ταῖς ψυχαῖς ;

426 Β : τοσοῦτον αὐτῇ κέντρον ὥσπερ μέλιττα ἐγκαταλέλοιπας (so Cobet).

Eunap. *Vit. Max.* 47 : τοσαύτη τις ἀφροδίτη τοῖς χείλεσιν ἐπεκάθητο.

Plato, *Laws*, 659 E:
καθάπερ τοῖς κάμνουσί τε καὶ ἀσθενῶς ἴσχουσι τὰ σώματα ἐν ἡδέσι τισὶ σιτίοις καὶ πώμασι τὴν χρηστὴν πειρῶνται τροφὴν προσφέρειν οἷς μέλει τούτων.

Himerius, *Or.* 5. 16:
ἀεὶ γάρ τις ἐπικαθίζει πειθὼ τοῖς χείλεσιν.

Eunap. *Vit. Chrys.* 112: τὸ ἀφελὲς ἐπεκάθητο τοῖς λόγοις ἥτε ἐπὶ τούτοις ἀφροδίτη τῶν ῥημάτων κατέθελγε τὸν ἀκροώμενον.

Themist. 330 A: λόγου δὲ κέντρον ἐγκαταλιπεῖν. 37 B.

Julian, 314 C: οὐκ οἶσθα ὅτι τὰ πικρὰ φάρμακα μιγνύντες οἱ ἰατροὶ τῷ μελικράτῳ προσφέρουσι;

Themist. 63 B: ἁπανταχοῦ δὲ τῷ κεχαρισμένῳ τὸ συμφέρον καταμιγνύναι ὥσπερ οἱ τῶν ἰατρῶν ἠπιώτεροι τὰ φάρμακα πρὸς τὴν αἴσθησιν ἐπικρύπτονται τοῖς ἡδύσμασι.

Themist. 302 B: τοὺς σοφωτέρους μιμητέον τῶν ἰατρῶν οἳ τὰ πικρότερα τῶν φαρμάκων μέλιτι τὴν κύλικα περιχρίσαντες πίνειν διδόασι.

Dio C. *Or.* 33. 10: ὅταν δέῃ τι τῶν ἀηδεστέρων πιεῖν,

Herod. *Thalia*.

προσφέρουσι μέλιτι χρίσασαι τὴν κύλικα.
Maximus Tyr. *Diss*. x. 6: οἱ ἰατροὶ τὰ πικρὰ τῶν φαρμάκων ἀναδεύσαντες προσηνεῖ τροφῇ κ.τ.λ.
Julian, 9 B: καὶ Κύρῳ.. οὐχ ὑπῆρχε τοῦτο· τελευτήσαντος γὰρ ὁ παῖς ὤφθη μακρῷ φαυλότερος ὥστε ὁ μὲν ἐκαλεῖτο πατὴρ ὁ δὲ ἐπωνομάσθη δεσπότης; and 85 D.
Themist. 233 A.
Dio C. *Or*. 4, p. 72, Arnim.

The illustration in 241 A seems to have been a common one; cf. that passage, ἐπεὶ καὶ τὴν μέλιτταν ἐκ τῆς δριμυτάτης πόας κ.τ.λ., with Psellus, Ep. 174 (Boiss.): ἡ μέλισσα ... καὶ τῷ θύμῳ προσίσταται. φυτὸν ὁ θύμος δριμύτατον κ.τ.λ.

The almost proverbial expression ταῖς μούσαις ᾄδω καὶ ἐμαυτῷ (*Misop*. 338) is found Themist. 366 B, Dio C. *Or*. 78. 420; cf. Burton, *Anatomy of Melancholy*, 'I have lived *mihi et Musis* in the University.'

The proverbial phrase τὸν ἔσχατον χιτῶνα ἀποδύσασθαι, 96 C, is not easy to trace to its source; cf. Dioscorides ap. Athen. 507 D: ἦν δὲ ὁ Πλάτων φιλόδοξος ὅστις ἔφησεν ἔσχατον τὸν τῆς δόξης χιτῶνα ἐν τῷ θανάτῳ αὐτῷ ἀποδυόμεθα, and ib. 281 D, with Tac. *Hist*. 4. 6: erant quibus Priscus appetentior famae videretur quando etiam sapientibus cupido gloriae novissima exuitur. The saying is, of course, not to be found in Plato.

For a modern use of the phrase cf. Chamfort, *Dialogues entre Saint-Réal, Epicure, Julien*, &c. : *Julien loq.* 'L'on sait que je ne fus pas insensible à la gloire ; c'est la dernière passion du sage ; c'est *la chemise de l'âme* m'a dit tout à l'heure un philosophe aimable, né parmi mes chers Gaulois. *Saint-Réal.* Ah ! je reconnais Montaigne.'—Chamfort, *Œuvres Choisies* (vol. i. p. 173 : *Bibliothèque Nationale*).

CHAPTER II

JULIAN'S RELATION TO PHILOSOPHY

JULIAN's relation to the philosophy of his day was that of an uncritical disciple, and he left nothing that can rank as a contribution to the doctrines of his school. He lived in a period of eclecticism, during which original speculation had practically ceased. The Neoplatonic was the only school of importance in the fourth Christian century, and Iamblichus, its chief representative, while he exaggerated certain aspects of its teaching, added little that was new. The Epicureans and Sceptics had fallen entirely into the background; the writings of their founders had already perished.[1] The Peripatatics had been merged in the Platonists and Neoplatonists.[2]

[1] Julian 301 c: μήτε 'Επικούρειος εἰσίτω λόγος μήτε Πυρρώνειος. ἤδη γὰρ καλῶς ποιοῦντες οἱ θεοὶ καὶ ἀνῃρήκασιν ὥστε ἐπιλείπειν καὶ τὰ πλεῖστα τῶν βιβλίων.

[2] The school was still recognised as having an independent existence; cf. S. Aug. *Contr. Acad.* iii. 19, 42 : nunc philosophos non fere videmus nisi aut Cynicos aut Peripateticos aut Platonicos ; but the position of Eugenius, Themistius' father, is probably typical of the Peripatetics who followed Alexander Aphrodisias (Zeller, vol. iv. p. 800). We gather from the references to Eugenius in Themistius that as a teacher of Aristotelian doctrines he held a prominent position. Constantius, in the panegyric of Themistius which is printed with the latter's Orations, speaks as follows of Eugenius,

Proclus, a century later, claimed to be the hierophant of all religions;[1] Iamblichus would have called himself a philosopher of all schools. But the eclecticism of the fourth century Neoplatonists was of the super-

Them. 23 A: ἐγγύθεν ὁ πατὴρ αὐτῷ, τίς δὲ οὗτός ἐστιν οὐδὲ ὑμεῖς ἀγνοεῖτε, οὗ τὸ ὄνομα εἰπόντι ἀπόχρη δεῖξαι τὴν ἀκροτάτην φιλοσοφίαν, καὶ οὔτε χῶρος οὔτε ἔθνος οὔτε πόλις οὐδεμία τῆς Εὐγενίου δόξης ἀνήκοος. Themistius himself declares that he owes his knowledge of philosophy to his father, Them. 240 D: δεῖ δὴ λοιπὸν τὰ ἴχνη τὰ σὰ διώκειν κ.τ.λ., cf. 244; Eugenius expounded Aristotle in the spirit of the later Peripatetics, who regarded it as a sacred duty to interpret his hidden meaning. Them. 235 A: τῆς σοφίας ἣν ἐκεῖνοι ... ἡμφίασεν ἀσαφείᾳ ... οὐ δὲ ἐγύμνους τὰ ἀγάλματα, cf. 294 D. In the Paraphrases, Themistius ἐπιχειρεῖ ἐξάγειν ἐκ τῶν ῥημάτων ἐν οἷς ἐκεῖνος αὐτὸν (τὸν νοῦν) καθεῖρξε ... τοῦ μὴ ἐπίδρομον εἶναι τοῖς ἀμυήτοις, cf. 319 et al. Paraphrases. Prooem. p. 2. 4. Sp.

From the language of Themistius it seems probable that these very Paraphrases, which brought him pupils in his lifetime and made him famous as an Aristotelian commentator, were founded on lectures delivered by his father, Them. 294 D: ἐμοὶ νέῳ ὄντι συγγράμματα ἅττα πεποίηται ἐν οἷς τὸν κλῆρον κατεθέμην καὶ ἐθησαύρισα ὃν παρὰ τῶν ἐμῶν πατέρων διεδεξάμην. Yet neither Eugenius nor Themistius can be considered pure Peripatetics. Eugenius followed the tendency of his day towards a reconciliation of Plato and Aristotle, Them. 236 A: πρὸς μὲν δὴ Πλάτωνα τὸν σόφον οὔτε αὐτός ποτε ἐστασίασεν οὔτε 'Αριστοτέλη ῥᾳδίως ᾤετο, 235 c: πολλάκις 'Αριστοτέλει προθύσας, εἰς τὴν Πλάτωνος ἔληγεν ἱερουργίαν. Themistius inclines to syncretism, 236 B: οὐδεμία γὰρ φιλοσοφία πόρρω ἀπῴκισται τῆς ἑτέρας. Cf. Simplic. De Cael. 33 B, 12: καὶ ὁ Θεμίστιος καί τοί γε ἐν τοῖς πλείστοις τὸν Περίπατον προϊσχόμενος, ἐν τούτῳ (the nature of the heavy and the light) τοῖς Πλάτωνος ἀρέσκεσθαι δοκεῖ μᾶλλον. Cf. Them. 27 A: 'Αριστοτέλους ὃν προυταξάμην τοῦ βίου τε καὶ τῆς σοφίας, with 366 c: Πλάτωνι συνὼν τῷ θεσπεσίῳ καὶ 'Αριστοτέλει συνδιαιτώμενος. Simplicius himself took the same attitude as Eugenius. Simplic. Cat. 2, δ: δεῖ δὲ οἶμαι καὶ τῶν πρὸς Πλάτωνα λεγομένων αὐτῷ (τῷ 'Αριστοτέλει) μὴ πρὸς τὴν λέξιν ἀποβλέποντα μόνον διαφωνίαν τῶν φιλοσόφων καταψηφίζεσθαι, ἀλλ' εἰς τὸν νοῦν ἀφορῶντα τὴν ἐν τοῖς πλείστοις συμφωνίαν αὐτῶν ἰχνεύειν.

[1] Marinus, Vit. Procl. c. 19: τὸν φιλόσοφον προσήκει (εἶναι) κοινῇ τοῦ ὅλου κόσμου ἱεροφάντην.

ficial, arbitrary sort. When a Platonic or an Aristotelian doctrine could be distorted or a phrase borrowed to help out his fantastic theories, Iamblichus claimed the authority of Plato or Aristotle.[1] Where Plato and Aristotle were at variance he did not scruple to force them into agreement. The final appeal, however, for Iamblichus and his followers was not to human wisdom but to divine revelation. 'The doctrines of Aristotle,' says Julian, 'are incomplete until they have been brought into harmony with those of Plato; and that is not enough: they must agree with the revelations granted by the gods.' In these words Julian summed up the philosophy of his day.

Neoplatonism, as compared with the rest of philosophy, was from the first religious. It is its effort to enlist philosophy in the service of practical religion that distinguishes fourth century Neoplatonism from the Neoplatonism of Plotinus and his forerunners. Plato's hints of mysticism were brought out and systematised by Plotinus. Plotinus, however, who had little faith in divination, and thought magic unworthy the philosopher, would have been slow to recognise his own speculations when they had passed through the hands of Iamblichus. The development worked out by the Syrian branch of the Neoplatonists was essential to the life of a school whose chief aim had come to be the promotion of Hellenism in the face of the rival attractions of Christianity, and the personal aberrations of Iamblichus

---

[1] Themistius hints at this tendency, 33 c: εἰ ἐγὼ μόνα δύο ῥήματα μεταβαλὼν καὶ μεθαρμόσας πρὸς ὑμᾶς ἀγροικιζοίμην οἷα τὰ πολλὰ εἰώθασιν οἱ νέοι Πλάτωνος θιασῶται; cf. *ib.* 295 B.

and his contemporaries should not be confused with Platonism as a whole. Such a generalisation as that made in the saying of Falconet—'Une secte où il falloit être fou de profession'[1]—shows a failure to appreciate the part played by the Neoplatonists in arousing and keeping alive an interest in philosophy during the last centuries of the Roman Empire. In an age which had no power to originate, which in philosophy, literature, and religion fell back on ancient models, third century Neoplatonism represents the only genuine revival. With Iamblichus began the decadence of Neoplatonism. For though we may decline to accept as history the story of his life as the credulous Eunapius tells it, we must admit that in him and his contemporaries we no longer find the severe spirituality that had marked the school of Plotinus.

Julian wished to make Neoplatonism the philosophy of the revived Hellenism, as Philo had tried to make the Platonic philosophy the philosophy of Judaism. He belonged by virtue of his date to the younger or Syrian branch of the school of which Iamblichus was the head and virtual founder. Plotinus he only once mentions, in passing; with the writings of Porphyry he does not seem to have been closely acquainted.[2] But of Iamblichus he always spoke with exaggerated respect,[3] ranked him with Plato,[4] and

[1] *Mém. Acad. Inscr.* vi. 517; cf. Lobeck, *Aglaoph.* pp. 91 sqq.
[2] Julian, 161 c.
[3] 222 B, δαιμόνιος; 146 B, ὁ κλεινὸς ἥρως. So Proclus never mentions Iamblichus without the epithet θεῖος, an honour which he does not pay to Plato.
[4] 146 A: τοῖς χρόνοις οὔ τι μὴν τῇ φύσει καταδεέστερον.

declared that he owed to his writings all his knowledge of speculative theology—the θεῶν γνῶσις,[1] which he 'would not exchange for the empire of the world.'[2] He tells his friend Sallust that he will find in Iamblichus τὸ τέλος τῆς ἀνθρωπίνης σοφίας.[3]

This fanatical devotion was inspired in Julian by a man whom historians have almost unanimously[4] condemned as an impostor, who disguised an unscrupulous practice of theurgy in the phrases of philosophy. That view has been based on the authority of Eunapius. But all that we absolutely know about the direction given by Iamblichus to Neoplatonism is that he brought it into touch with the religions of the East, which, in the fourth century, were more popular than ever, and that the Neoplatonists who followed him were rather priests than philosophers.[5] Theurgy,

[1] 146 B.
[2] 222 B.
[3] 157 C. Cf. Julian, *Frag.* 6: καὶ ὁ κλεινὸς ἡμῖν ἔδειξε καὶ ἱεροφάντης Ἰάμβλιχος.
[4] Kirchner, *Die Philosophie des Plotin*, p. 216, is the only important exception. He considers that the transcendentalism of Iamblichus must have saved him from the vulgarities of theurgy, and regards the stories of Eunapius as pure fiction, but does not attempt to explain away the evidences of belief in supernatural manifestations which can be found in the writings of Iamblichus himself. The *De Mysteriis* has been rejected by Zeller, v. p. 716, on account of its style. The *Life of Pythagoras* remains; in the Προτρεπτικὸς and the Commentary of Proclus *in Timaeum*, the chief source of the opinions of Iamblichus, there is little trace of superstition. But Photius, *Cod.* p. 173, mentions a work by I. Philoponus, attacking the treatise of Iamblichus περὶ ἀγαλμάτων. Iamblichus had defended the theory that certain images had fallen from heaven, πολλὰ μὲν ἀπίθανα μυθολογῶν, πολλὰ δὲ εἰς ἀδήλους φέρων αἰτίας, πολλὰ δὲ καὶ τοῖς ὁρωμένοις ἐναντία γράφειν οὐκ αἰσχυνόμενος. Cf. Photius, p. 337.
[5] Vacherot, *L'École d'Alexandrie*, p. 67, and cf. the saying of

as it was understood in the fourth century, had for its aim the perfection of the spirit and the purification of the soul of the initiated, through αὐτοψία. To distinguish between self-delusion and imposture, in such a case, is not easy, and, in the present state of the evidence, it seems impossible to decide whether Iamblichus was a mystical fanatic or an impostor of much the same type as Lucian's Alexander, though more refined in his methods. That it was precisely this mixture of religious mysticism and philosophy that appealed to Julian's tastes we may be sure from the fact that it was not to the Roman senate and aristocracy, then the real strongholds of Paganism, that he turned for sympathy, but to the Sophists of Athens and Antioch. Beugnot[1] remarks on this as a fault of diplomacy, and Boissier[2] regards the narrow Hellenism which prevented his enlisting Rome and the West to aid in his religious revival as one of the causes of Julian's failure. But Julian was too genuinely an enthusiast to have been content with a religion of forms, maintained for political purposes and unsupported by a solid basis of his favourite Platonic philosophy.

It has been usual for the biographers of Julian to accept without reservation the story told by Eunapius of his relations with the representatives of

Proclus quoted *supra*. Libanius, *Panegyr.*, says that Julian surpassed the priests of Egypt in his knowledge of sacred things; cf. *ib.* ii. p. 56 (of Julian): ἐν τελεταῖς μυρίαις ὁμιλήσας δαίμοσι. Julian himself, 180 B, prays for ἐν θεουργίᾳ τελειότητα.

[1] *Destruction du Paganisme*, i. p. 216.
[2] *La fin du Paganisme*, i. p. 94. Julian's natural preference for Eastern doctrines is further shown by the fact that he regarded even the Greeks as outsiders in religious matters, 147 A.

the Neoplatonic school at Pergamum and Ephesus. He relates that Aedesius, the successor of Iamblichus, himself grown too infirm to teach, handed over the youthful Julian to Chrysanthius and Eusebius, his pupils, telling him, in words which recall the asceticism of Porphyry, that, once initiated into their mysteries, he would blush to own a body.[1] Eusebius seems to have been the only one of the small band of the followers of Iamblichus to rate speculation (τὰς μηχανὰς διαλεκτικάς) above theurgy (τὰ θαυματοποιῶν ἔργα).[2] But his warnings against theurgy and the absent Maximus[3] only inflamed Julian's curiosity, which was fed by the miraculous tales told by Chrysanthius. Julian repudiated the abstract teaching of Eusebius, and hastened to Ephesus, to be initiated by Maximus into the mysteries of αὐτοψία.

However reluctant we may be to admit the evidence of so credulous and superficial a biographer as Eunapius, we cannot deny that the outlines of his story agree with the independent versions of Libanius,[4] and of Julian himself. Maximus wrote nothing from which we might rehabilitate him, and we must leave him to his biographer. It was

[1] Eunap. *Vit. Max.* 48–52.
[2] Eunap. *loc. cit.*
[3] For the reputation of Maximus, at this time, see Libanius, *Or.* i. p. 528: τῆς φήμης πανταχοῖ φερομένης πάντες οἱ περὶ τὰς Μούσας καὶ τοὺς ἄλλους γε θεοὺς, οἱ μὲν ὡδοιπόρουν, οἱ δ' ἔπλεον, σπεύδοντες ἰδεῖν τε ἐκεῖνον καὶ συγγενέσθαι καὶ εἰπεῖν αὐτοί τε καὶ ἀκοῦσαι λέγοντος.
[4] Liban. *Or. parent.* § 9: καί ποτε τοῖς τοῦ Πλάτωνος γέμουσιν εἰς ταὐτὸν ἐλθών, ἀκούσας ὑπέρ τε θεῶν καὶ δαιμόνων, ... καὶ τί τε ἡ ψυχὴ καὶ πόθεν ἥκει .... ἁλμυρὰν ἀκοὴν ἀπεκλύσατο τῷ ποτίμῳ λόγῳ κ.τ.λ.

JULIAN'S RELATION TO PHILOSOPHY 45

to his influence that Julian's friends attributed the final conversion to Hellenism which took place about his twentieth year,[1] and Julian's writings testify to his lasting admiration of both Maximus and Chrysanthius.[2] All, then, that remains for the student of Julian, when he has pointed out the untrustworthiness of Eunapius, is to examine those passages in Julian's works which show signs of the superstition which, on the strength of Eunapius, has always been associated with his name.[3]

Of Julian's conviction that an uncritical belief in the old national religion was not merely expedient but absolutely essential for the preservation of Hellenic culture and the maintenance of the Roman Empire, there can be no question. His vague ideal had been the restoration of the old gods of Greece, but when he

---

[1] Liban. *Ep.* 606 (To Maximus): οἶμαι δὲ καὶ πάντας ὀφείλειν σοι χάριν· κοινὸς γὰρ εὐεργέτης σὺ γῆς τε καὶ θαλάττης . . . θρέψας ἡμῖν καὶ δημιουργήσας βασιλέα πάντα ἄκρον. Cf. Gregor. Naz. *Or.* iii. p. 61 D: Ἀσία ἦν αὐτῷ τὸ τῆς ἀσεβείας διδασκαλεῖον . . . ἐπεὶ δὲ ἤδη τῶν ἐν φιλοσοφίᾳ δογμάτων ἥψατο καὶ τὴν ἐκ τοῦ λόγου προσελάμβανε δύναμιν οὐκέτι κατέχειν ὅλην τὴν νόσον οἷός τε ἦν, and Liban. i. 528. Libanius congratulates Maximus on his influence over Julian, *Paneg.* i. p. 376.

[2] Amm. Marc. 22, 7, 3; 25, 3, 23. Of the four letters addressed to Maximus by Julian, two have been rejected by Cumont and Schwarz; *Ep.* 16, on insufficient grounds (see *Appendix* i.) But, at any rate, *Epp.* 38, 39 are left to prove Julian's admiration for Maximus.

[3] See Aurelius Victor, *Epit.* 152, cultus numinum superstitiosus; and Ammian, superstitiosus magis quam legitimus sacrorum observator; in both of which passages, however, it should be noted that *superstitiosus* was applied by the Romans to one whose observance of religion was considered excessive, *e.g.* Marcus Aurelius, and thus had a slightly different connotation from its English equivalent.

had fairly faced their numbers and given them back their special altars and sacrifices, the Platonist revolted in his blood. He recognised that for philosophers and men of letters the old simple faith in the gods of Homer could never take the place of the monotheism that philosophy had been teaching for centuries. But he was all the more sensitive as to the attitude of the people towards the individual gods and the legends of the poets.[1] In public there must be no hint of impiety ὅπως μὴ τῷ πλήθει τῆς τοιαύτης ἀρχηγοὶ θρασύτητος γενώμεθα.[2] After relating with edifying piety the miraculous story of the arrival at Rome of the Mother of the Gods, he adds καίτοι με οὐ λέληθεν ὅτι φήσουσιν αὐτά τινες τῶν λίαν σοφῶν ὕθλους εἶναι γραδίων οὐκ ἀνεκτούς. ἐμοὶ δὲ δοκεῖ ταῖς πόλεσι πιστεύειν μᾶλλον τὰ τοιαῦτα ἢ τούτοισι τοῖς κομψοῖς ὧν τὸ ψυχάριον δριμὺ μὲν ὑγιὲς δὲ οὐδὲ ἓν βλέπει.[3]

Whatever may have been Julian's private and philosophic uncertainties as to the grounds of his religious creed, he never expressed them. The use of the argument from expediency in such a passage as that just quoted, unsupported as it is by any positive reservations, is not enough to justify a doubt as to his personal faith. The positive evidence points the

---

[1] He approves of Plato's expression of belief in the popular gods: πιστεύειν γὰρ ἁπλῶς ἀξιοῖ καὶ χωρὶς ἀποδείξεως λεγομένοις, ὅσα ὑπὲρ τῶν θεῶν φασιν οἱ ποιηταί, 237 B; without, however, recognising that the Platonic passage of which he is thinking (*Timaeus*, 40) was meant to be ironical.

[2] Hence his indignation with οἱ δυσσεβέστατοι ἀνθρώπων, who laugh at the prohibition of certain foods, during the Mysteries.

[3] 161 B. For similar expressions, see 212 B,C, 222 C, 180 B *et al*. For the passage in 161 B quoted above see reminiscences from the *Republic* of Plato, *infra*, chap. iii. p. 77.

other way. Ammianus tells us that Julian consulted the entrails at every crisis, and for his belief in signs from heaven we have his own testimony. In every case of doubt or difficulty there came to him, not merely the negative guidance [1] granted to Socrates, but positive encouragement and promises.[2] Zeus thunders on the right for Julian as often as for any Homeric hero.[3]

One of the ways in which philosophy had tried to reconcile polytheism with its own belief in the unity of God was the theory of demons. This effort to relate the gods and the world was made as early as Hesiod, though its interest for philosophy does not begin till Plutarch developed the theory from Plato.[4] It paved the way for the marvellous in religion and philosophy, and that alone was enough to secure its popularity in the early Christian centuries. As a Neoplatonist, Julian believes in demons, good and bad; for it was one of the inconsistencies of the Neo-platonists that, while they refused to believe that God could be the cause of evil, they recognised evil demons

---

[1] 275 D the gods warn him not to send a letter to Eusebia; 284 C he has a sign not to oppose the troops; cf. Zosim. iii. 9 for his vision at Vienna.

[2] 361 C the statue in the temple of Apollo gave him a sign, as he called Helios to witness; 286 D γενομένων καλῶν τῶν ἱερῶν; 399 D the gods bid him sacrifice, and promise rewards; 415 D.

[3] Even Libanius, who was himself singularly free from superstition, encouraged Julian to think he had visions and direct help from the gods; i. 460.

[4] Plut. *de I. et O.* 560 ascribes the theory to Plato, Pythagoras &c., but cf. Hesiod, *O. et D.* 120, and see Plato, *Sympos.* 23, Plut. *de def. orac.* 421, 314, *de Is.* 136, Lobeck, *Aglaoph.* p. 696. Apuleius did much to make it popular, *de deo Socr.* 6, *et al.*

as divine agencies.¹ The sun, he says, gives power to angels and demons;² some men are driven by wicked demons into the desert,³ or pursued by them on account of neglect of temple-worship.

Julian believed, with the Neoplatonists, that the soul of man is imprisoned in its earthly body, to expiate a fall;⁴ that matter is evil, and that the effort of one's life should be to flee from it;⁵ that on the success of this effort all happiness depends.⁶ But this is not all. If Julian had stopped here, as Plato had done, he would have separated himself from his century and his school. It was here that Neoplatonism joined hands with religion. This ἀπαθανατισμὸς τῆς ψυχῆς (Procl. *in Tim.* 5, 39, 1) is reached by knowledge of the gods;⁷ and this knowledge is attained in the state of ecstasy,⁸ the ecstasy of Plotinus.⁹ Julian

---

[1] Julian sacrificed to the demons of the night, Liban. *Paneg.*
[2] 145 c.
[3] 288 B; cf. Plut. *de I. et O.* 561: ὁ Ξενοκράτης οἴεται εἶναι φύσεις ἐν τῷ περιέχοντι μεγάλας μὲν καὶ ἰσχυράς, δυστρόπους δὲ καὶ σκυθρωπὰς αἳ χαίρουσι τοῖς τοιούτοις; 288 A. With Julian's theory of a demon in us cf. Iamblich. *Protrep.* 12. 17: ἡμεῖς τὸν δαίμονα αἱρούμεθα κ.τ.λ., and *ib.* 15. 2: ὁ δοθεὶς καὶ συγκληρωθεὶς ἡμῖν ἀπὸ τῶν θεῶν δαίμων.
[4] 198 B: τὸν τῆς ψυχῆς δεσμόν; cf. Iamblich. *Protrep.* c. iii. p. 11 κωλύεται ὥστε μὴ δύνασθαι ῥᾳδίως ἐξιέναι καὶ τῶν δεσμῶν ἀπολύεσθαι; Julian, 169 c: οὐρανόθεν ἔπτημεν εἰς τὴν γῆν καὶ ἐπέσομεν.
[5] 166 c; 248 B.
[6] 194-7; 180 B: δίδου πᾶσι μὲν ἀνθρώποις εὐδαιμονίαν ἧς τὸ κεφάλαιον ἡ τῶν θεῶν γνῶσίς ἐστιν.
[7] 218 A; 221 D.
[8] 178 B: ὅταν γὰρ ἡ ψυχὴ πᾶσαν ἑαυτὴν δῷ τοῖς θεοῖς, ὅλα τὰ καθ' ἑαυτὴν ἐπιτρέψασα τοῖς κρείττοσιν . . . ὄντος οὐδενὸς λοιπὸν τοῦ ἀπείργοντος καὶ ἐμποδίζοντος . . . αὐτίκα μὲν αὐταῖς ἐλλάμπει τὸ φῶς.
[9] With Julian, *loc. cit.*, cf. Plotinus, *Enn.* vi. 9, 9, 10: ὁρᾶν δὴ ἔστιν ἐνταῦθα κἀκεῖνον καὶ ἑαυτὸν ὡς ὁρᾶν θέμις, ἑαυτὸν μὲν ἠγλαϊσμένον,

describes it as a sort of Bacchic frenzy[1] reserved for the initiated.[2] Without this delirious enthusiasm life is thrown away, because deprived of the θεῶν γνῶσις.[3] It is always in the language of the Mysteries that Julian speaks of things divine, which are, for him, the highest philosophy.[4] The greatest boon he can ask of the gods is proficiency in the hidden things of the Mysteries,[5] initiation into which Iamblichus had thought essential for the Neoplatonic philosopher.[6] He speaks in veiled language, from the standpoint of the initiated, and is always on the brink of revealing, but never reveals, the secret doctrines unintelligible to the crowd, θεουργοῖς δὲ τοῖς μακαρίοις γνώριμα.[7] Yet from such phraseology as this it would be unfair to argue superstition. Allusions to the mysteries and metaphors borrowed from them are common in Greek literature from Plato down. The language of initiation was used especially with reference to philosophic doctrines, and we have met with it even in a writer as free from superstition as Themistius.[8]

φωτὸς πλήρη νοητοῦ—φῶς αὐτὸ καθαρὸν .... ἔσται δὲ ὅτε καὶ τὸ συνεχὲς ἔσται τῆς θέας οὐκέτι ἐνοχλουμένῳ.

[1] 221 D: ἴστω Διόνυσος αὐτὸς ᾧ καὶ προσεύχομαι τάς τε ἐμὰς καὶ τὰς ὑμετέρας ἐκβακχεῦσαι φρένας ἐπὶ τὴν ἀληθῆ τῶν θεῶν γνῶσιν.
[2] 218 A: ὑμῶν τοῖς πολλοῖς ὅσοι τέως ἐστὲ τούτων ἀμύητοι τὴν ὄνησιν δοῖεν.
[3] 222 A; 172 D; cf. Iambl. Protr. iii. 11, 15.
[4] 223 A.
[5] 180 B.
[6] 237 D.
[7] 172 D: ἄγνωπτα ἐρῶ τῷ συρφετῷ; 218 A: βοῦν ἐπὶ τῇ γλώττῃ—περὶ γὰρ τῶν ἀρρήτων οὐδὲν χρὴ λέγειν; cf. 174 D, 159 A, 148 A, 152 B, 185 C, 157 D, 239 A.
[8] Themist. 2 B, 235 A, 71 A; Damasc. Vit. Isid. ap. Photius, 337:

Iamblichus and his followers believed in the possibility of a visible revelation of the gods.[1] Julian's references to theurgy are, as a rule, too vague for us to be able to decide as to his attitude to such miraculous manifestations. A passage in his seventh oration seems at first sight to indicate a belief in them. He is expounding the hidden truths of the Heracles myth, and his language throughout is confused and contradictory. He is indignant with those who interpret literally the tale of the birth of Heracles and his earthly career in human form. Heracles is indeed the son of Zeus in the sense in which Athene is his daughter, as a $δύναμις$ emanating from him,[2] but Julian will not admit the human element.[3] As for the adventures of his childhood, $ταῦτα\ μὲν\ ὑπῆρξε, μειζόνως\ δὲ\ ἢ\ κατ'\ ἄνθρωπον$. 'They say,' continues Julian, 'that Heracles crossed the sea in a golden bowl, but my belief is that he walked on the waters. To Heracles all things are possible.'[4] Zeller[5] quotes

$τέλος\ ἔχειν\ ἤλπιζεν\ εἰ\ τῆς\ Πλάτωνος\ διανοίας\ εἴσω\ τῶν\ ἀδύτων\ δυνηθείη\ διαβαλεῖν$. Perhaps the best example in Plato is *Phaedrus*, 250 B; cf. Lobeck, *Aglaoph.* 57 : Etenim Plato in Phaedro cum docere vellet quantum oblectationis habeat inquisitio et investigatio veri ($ἡ\ τῶν\ ὄντως\ ὄντων\ θέα$) exemplum sumit a mysteriis contenditque animos e rerum superarum immutabiliumque cognitione plus voluptatis capere quam divinae species initiatis afferant.

[1] *Auct. de Myst.* i. 8.
[2] See *infra* and 149 B.
[3] Julian in his philosophical writings is usually a strong opponent of anthropomorphism, though we can hardly say with Naville 'L'anthropomorphisme lui est tout à fait étranger ;' cf. the assertion of 219 B and 82 D, the $θεῶν\ γένη$ are $ἀφανῆ\ αἰσθήσει\ καὶ\ ἀνέφικτα$, discerned with difficulty even by the kindred $νοῦς$, with *contra Chr.* 200 A, where Asclepius assumes the human form.
[4] 219 D.
[5] *Phil. der Griech.* v. p. 720.

the passage to illustrate the belief of Iamblichus and his school in visible revelation. But Julian goes on: 'For all the elements bow down before the demiurgic and efficient power of that pure and undying intelligence which Zeus made to descend to earth by the aid of Athene.' By making Heracles a δύναμις, Julian seems to put out of question the physical appearances of the legend.[1] Julian's treatment of the Dionysus legend (221) leaves the reader altogether in doubt as to whether he believed in the actual manifestation of the god on earth.

It is easy enough to find such inconsistencies in Julian's religious professions. 'Peut-on concevoir,' says Beugnot,[2] 'que le même homme qui sacrifiait avec une visible dévotion ait dit que les simulacres étaient faits non pour qu'on les regardât comme des dieux, mais afin d'exciter les·hommes à la piété? C'est que toutes les idées de Julien n'étaient point encore fixées. Si sa jeunesse ne devait pas lui servir d'excuse, on trouverait dans l'état de la philosophie païenne au quatrième siècle de suffisants motifs pour l'absoudre.' To this we may add that what is true of most of the Neoplatonists, from Plotinus to Proclus, remains true for Julian. In his personal conduct he may have been carried away by the prevailing interest in theurgy and the Mysteries. But the spiritual character of the Neoplatonic philosophy that had

---

[1] Professor Shorey suggests that the parenthesis ἦν . . . νενόμικα 219 D is a passing sneer at the Christians, and should not be taken too seriously; and has pointed out another possible sneer in 144 B: γεννᾷ μὲν ἐν κόσμῳ τὸν Ἀσκληπιόν, ἔχει δὲ αὐτὸν καὶ πρὸ τοῦ κόσμου παρ' ἑαυτῷ.

[2] *Destruction du Paganisme*, i. 209.

raised Plotinus above the superstitions of his day had been sufficiently preserved in the fourth century to save its followers from embodying the grosser forms of that superstition in their writings.

Julian's writings, as has been said, hardly rank as a contribution to Neoplatonism. But his two philosophical Orations serve as good illustrations of ὕμνοι φυσικοί,[1] and one of them (*Or.* 4) perhaps supplies the place of a lost treatise of Iamblichus (περὶ θεῶν), of which it may have been little more than a copy.[2] Like all the Neoplatonists, Iamblichus had built his theories round the framework of a trinity.[3] Julian follows him in the main with his trinity of the κόσμος ὁρατός, or visible universe,[4] the κόσμος νοερὸς, its model, relieved from the imperfections of matter, and represented in the ὁρατὸν by the planets, and, thirdly, the κόσμος νοητὸς, over which rules the supreme principle of the Good, or the One (τὸ ἕν) not to be grasped by the intelligence.

Julian's ὕμνος was not meant to be a complete

[1] See Menander's definition apud Spengel, *Rhetores Graeci*, iii.: εἰσὶ δὲ τοιοῦτοι (φυσικοὶ) ὕμνοι ὅταν 'Απόλλωνος ὕμνον λέγοντες ἥλιον αὐτὸν εἶναι φάσκωμεν, καὶ περὶ τοῦ ἡλίου τῆς φύσεως διαλεγώμεθα κ.τ.λ.

[2] Julian, 150 D, 157 D; Iambl. *Protr.* p. 120; *Festa et Pistelli*; *Auct. de Myst.* viii. 8.

[3] Or, rather, a series of trinities. For, as their transcendental conceptions of the spiritual world removed it further from the world of sense, the Neoplatonists needed to multiply such media, in order to maintain the relation between the two.

[4] Julian's trinity has been thoroughly treated by Zeller and others, especially by M. A. Naville, *L'empereur Julien et la philosophie du polythéisme*; a work which has rendered superfluous any further treatment of this part of Julian's philosophy. Only a brief outline, therefore, will be given here, for the sake of completeness.

JULIAN'S RELATION TO PHILOSOPHY

exposition of the theology of the school; his main object was the glorification of his favourite deity—the Sun. He tells us that he was born a sun-worshipper;[1] of his peculiar calling to follow in the Sun's[2] train he has private proofs, which, with an affectation of τὸ σεμνὸν, caught from the Neoplatonists,[3] he will not reveal.[4] His devotion was spontaneous; the state of ecstasy into which it threw him had not been inspired by books.[5] Sun-worship was no new thing in the Roman Empire, and, for Roman Emperors, the cult had had a special attraction, from the days when Augustus built his temple to the Palatine Apollo, and Nero tried to identify himself with the god. As the Roman Empire came into closer contact with Oriental beliefs, the cult became more and more popular, and,

---

[1] 130 c, cf. Amm. Marc. xxii. 5, 1: a rudimentis pueritiae primis, inclinatior erat erga numinum cultum. Cf. Liban. i. 375: τὴν μὲν διάνοιαν ὑψηλοτέραν ποιῶν τῇ τῶν οὐρανίων μαθήσει. Allusions to the Pythagorean doctrine of the importance of the θεωρία τοῦ οὐρανοῦ are frequent in Neoplatonic literature. Iambl. *Protr.* p. 12: ἡ μετὰ ταύτην γνώμη (of Pythagoras) ποιεῖται τὴν παράκλησιν καὶ πᾶσαν τὴν περὶ τὸν οὐρανὸν θεωρίαν, and *ibid.* p. 115: φιλοσόφει τὸν οὐρανὸν ὁρῶν καὶ τὸν ἥλιον, φῶς τέ σοι τῆς ἀληθείας ἡγείσθω, ἐπὶ θεοὺς δὲ καὶ σοφίαν διὰ τῆς τῶν οὐρανίων ἐπισκέψεως ἀνέρχου. Cf. Julian, 143 B: ἄκουε δὴ πρῶτον ὅσα φασὶν οἱ τὸν οὐρανὸν οὐχ ὥσπερ ἵπποι καὶ βόες ὁρῶντες ἀλλ' ἐξ αὐτοῦ τὴν ἀφανῆ πολυπραγμονοῦντες φύσιν, and 148 c. And, for the Platonic authority which Julian and Iamblichus may have had in mind, *Timaeus* 47 A: ὄψις—αἰτία τῆς μεγίστης ὠφελείας ἡμῖν, ὅτι τῶν νῦν λόγων ... οὐδεὶς ἄν ποτε ἐρρήθη μήτε ἄστρα μήτε ἥλιον μήτε οὐρανὸν ἰδόντων, κ.τ.λ.

[2] Ἡλίου ὀπαδός.

[3] Cf. Iambl. *Protr.* 21, p. 106, on Pythagorean maxims: τὰ παρ' αὐτοῖς ἀπόρρητα, καὶ ἐχεμυθούμενα πρὸς τοὺς ἀνεισάκτους παραλιπόντες ἀνεξέταστα.

[4] 130 c.

[5] 131 A.

finally, Aurelian established games in the Sun's honour at Rome, and traced his parentage to the Sun-god.[1] The identification of the Sun with Apollo is found throughout Greek literature, but, for Sun-worship as Julian conceived it, he could not go to Greek sources; it is to specifically Eastern influence that we must trace the peculiar form of worship that we find in the third and fourth centuries of the Roman Empire. That influence is marked by the introduction of the name Mithras. Mithras-worship first makes its appearance among the Romans towards the end of the Republic, in the time of Pompeius.[2] But, while the cults of Isis and Serapis had been received with all the hospitality that the Romans extended to new deities, the Mithras cult gained ground slowly, and not till the time of Hadrian and the Antonines had it secured an equal footing with the others. Thenceforward, however, it gradually overpowered them, and soon contested the supremacy with Zeus himself.[3] Julian worships his Sun-god under the name of Mithras.

One of the objects of his ὕμνος was to show the

[1] Preller, *Myth.* ii. p. 408; Julian, 156 B, speaking of the feriæ Soli invicto: ποιοῦμεν ἡλίῳ τὸν περιφανέστατον ἀγῶνα τὴν ἑορτὴν Ἡλίῳ καταφημίσαντες ἀνικήτῳ.

[2] Plut. *Vit. Pomp.* 24. The pirates of Cilicia τελετάς τινας ἀπορρήτους ἐτέλουν ὧν ἡ τοῦ Μίθρου καὶ μέχρι δεῦρο διασώζεται καταδειχθεῖσα πρῶτον ὑπ' ἐκείνων. Because in certain of its rites the Mithras cult recalled the sacraments of the Christian Church, Tertullian called it a 'Satanic plagiarism of Christianity.' Cf. Beugnot, i. p. 58.

[3] Boissier, *La Religion Romaine*, p. 383, Julian, 155 B: εἴ σοι μετὰ τοῦτο φαίην ὡς καὶ τὸν Μίθραν τιμῶμεν καὶ ἄγομεν Ἡλίῳ τετραετηρικοὺς ἀγῶνας, ἐρῶ νεώτερα. Julian speaks scornfully of the ignorant Greek attitude to Eastern doctrines, 147 A: ἀξύνετον ἴσως λέγω τοῖς Ἕλλησιν ὥσπερ δέον μόνον τὰ συνήθη καὶ γνώριμα λέγειν ... ὦ σοφώτατοι καὶ ἀβασανίστως τὰ πολλὰ παραδεχόμενοι.

unity of Hellenic and Oriental religions, and here he was in harmony with the monotheistic teaching of his age. The identification of deities, Hellenic, Roman, and Eastern, had been going on for centuries, and the Neoplatonists, in their effort to reconcile theism and polytheism in their theology, naturally pushed the tendency to its furthest limits. Apuleius [1] shows us how far this unifying process had been carried in the second century. This doctrine of *imperium penes unum, officia penes multos*, which dates back to the Stoics,[2] is carefully elaborated by Julian in order to secure the supremacy for his favourite Helios.[3] He followed Plotinus and Iamblichus in making the supreme principle the ἓν or ἀγαθὸν, more transcendental than Plato's ἀγαθὸν, because no longer identified with, or rather on the same plane with, νοῦς,[4] though like the Platonic ἀγαθὸν it presides over the νοητὸς κόσμος, where rule the Intelligible Gods, the Ideas.[5]

Next in rank to these νοητοὶ θεοὶ, whom Julian leaves as vague as the Platonic Ideas, come the

[1] Apul. *Metam.* xi. 5.
[2] Servius ad Verg. *Georg.* i. 5 : Stoici dicunt non esse nisi unum deum et unam eandemque potestatem, quae, pro ratione officiorum nostrorum, variis nominibus appellatur.
[3] For the identification of the Sun with other deities see Macrob. *Sat.* i. 17, 4 : diversae virtutes solis nomina dis dederunt; and the whole chapter.
[4] For this, the conventional view of the relation of νοῦς and τὸ ἀγαθὸν in Plato, see Zeller v. 476 *et al.*; and for a wholly different interpretation, see Professor Shorey, in the *University of Chicago Classical Studies*, i. 188, note.
[5] The notion of classified gods, νοητοὶ and νοεροί, was imported into the Neoplatonic system by Iamblichus. Cf. Kirchner, *Die Phil. des Plotin*, p. 212; *Auct. de Myst.* 8, 8, p. 271, *Parthey*; δύο γένη περικοσμίων τε καὶ ὑπερκοσμίων θεῶν κ.τ.λ.

νοεροὶ θεοί, in whom the faculty of νοῦς is both active and passive as bestowed by the Sun.[1] He is the chief νοερὸς θεὸς, and, as such, is the object of Julian's adoration. The material Sun, which we see, is an image of him, as the visible planets are images of the νοητοὶ θεοί.[2]

Julian had Platonic authority for making the Sun the ἀγαθοῦ ἔκγονος,[3] and a god,[4] and for giving him a soul.[5] He disposes of the ἀγαθὸν and the νοητὸς κόσμος in a few words and devotes the rest of his exposition to the Sun. The three members of his trinity were sharply divided. The Sun furnished the link that relates them to one another (συνοχή τις). Inasmuch as he is the link between the immaterial κόσμοι and again between them and the world of sense, his μεσότης is not one of place alone, but of influence; he is the unifier.[6]

---

[1] 145 B : τοῖς νοεροῖς τὸ νοεῖν καὶ νοεῖσθαι παρέχει.
[2] *Contr. Christ.* 65 B (Neumann); cf. Boissier, p. 111, Naville, p. 101.
[3] *Rep.* 508 B, 506 D, *et al.*
[4] *Rep.* 508 A.
[5] Plat. *Laws*, 967 : for the analogy of the Sun in Neoplatonic doctrines, see Iamblich. *Protrep.* p. 17 : ἀπὸ τῶν γνωρίμων . . . δι' ἀναλογίας ἐναργοῦς . . . τὸ τὸν ἥλιον τῶν ἄστρων ὑπερέχειν, οὐδένα λέληθε, καὶ τὸ τὸν νοῦν τῆς ψυχῆς εἶναι ἐξάρχοντα κ.τ.λ.
[6] μεσότης is the regular Aristotelian word for the mean; and has a local, temporal, and ethical significance. But there is no evidence that it was used in the active sense of 'mediator' before Julian. There is a curious passage in Plutarch, which seems to indicate that the local μεσότης of the Sun was a Persian doctrine. *De I. et O.* 46 : καὶ προσαπεφαίνετο τὸν μὲν (the principle of good) ἐοικέναι φωτὶ μάλιστα τῶν αἰσθητῶν, τὸν δ' (the principle of evil) ἔμπαλιν σκότῳ καὶ ἀγνοίᾳ, μέσον δὲ ἀμφοῖν τὸν Μίθρην εἶναι. διὸ καὶ Μίθρην Πέρσαι τὸν Μεσίτην ὀνομάζουσιν. Now μεσότης is the New Testament word for 'mediator,' and is so used by Polybius, Diodorus, and Philo. Possibly, therefore, there may be more than a local μεσότης indicated

To what extent Julian borrowed from Iamblichus the details of the numerous μεσότητες[1] of the Sun, we cannot decide. But we learn from Proclus[2] that Iamblichus had written of the middle term of one of his intellectual triads in much the same words as Julian uses of the Sun. To the νοερὸς κόσμος the Sun gives the unity, harmony, and intelligence that he has received from the ἀγαθόν. For the visible world he is the sole source of light and order. The ἕν or ἀγαθόν is too remote for adoration, and Julian's system results in a practically monotheistic worship of Helios.

But Julian's revival was in the name of polytheism, and if he could not restore, in the fourth Christian century, the old naïve faith in the gods of Homer, he nevertheless could not omit from his creed the numerous deities whose temples and altars he had rebuilt. The world of Hellenism, for which he wrote, was no longer content with deities whose nature it did not know, and for whose actions it could not account.

in the Plutarch passage. M. Naville has pointed out the resemblance between the Sun as mediator and the Christian Λόγος, which Julian may have had in mind, and we may add Philo, De Somn. 586 D: ὅτι τοῖς ἐπικήροις ἡμῖν συνέφερε μεσίταις καὶ διαιτηταῖς λόγοις χρῆσθαι.

[1] 142 A: ἐν μέσοις τεταγμένος κατὰ παντοίαν μεσότητα ... τελειότητος καὶ συνοχῆς καὶ γονίμου ζωῆς καὶ τῆς ἐνοειδοῦς οὐσίας τὰ μέσα ἔχων ἐν ἑαυτῷ. Proclus in Tim. 259 D, quoting Iamblichus, uses phraseology which strongly resembles Julian's.

[2] Procl. in Tim. 94 c. In this triad νοῦς comes first, τοῦ δὲ μέσου καὶ τὴν συμπλήρωσιν συνάγοντος τῶν τοιούτων τὸ γόνιμον τῶν θεῶν καὶ τὸ συναγωγὸν τῶν τριῶν καὶ τὸ τῆς ἐνεργείας ἀποπληρωτικὸν καὶ τὸ προϊὸν παντὶ καὶ τὸ ἀγαθουργὸν μάλιστα δείγματα λέγουσι. Cf. Zeller, v. p. 691. Other passages in Proclus which seem to prove that Julian followed the phraseology of Iamblichus are In Tim. 297 c, 140 c, 49 c (cf. Julian, 153 B and 144 D), 94 B, and especially In Tim. 292 E, F.

Here Julian took advantage of the syncretism, which, as has been earlier indicated, had been going on for centuries. The old names, endeared by the associations of Greek and Latin literature, could be retained without endangering the supremacy of Helios. Julian identified Zeus, Helios, Hades,[1] and Serapis.[2] It is evident at once how far he had strayed from Homer. The omnipotent Zeus of Greek mythology is degraded to a $\delta\eta\mu\iota o\nu\rho\gamma\iota\kappa\grave{\eta}$ $\delta\acute{\nu}\nu\alpha\mu\iota s$[3] which works with Helios, and has no separate existence.[4] Homer is quoted to prove the identity of Helios and Oceanus.[5] Tradition had made Athene the child of Zeus. Julian rejects the ordinary version, and regards her as the manifestation of the intelligent forethought[6] of Helios, identified with Zeus, as Dionysus is the vehicle of his fairest thoughts,[7] and Aphrodite the principle that, emanating from him, charms and gives life to matter.[8] Julian did not forget the gods of Egypt; places had been assigned to Mithras and

[1] 136 A. Cf. *Phaedo*, 80 D, and *Cratylus*, 403 E, passages not meant to be entirely serious.

[2] Cf. *Ep.* 10. 378 : ἡμῶν οὓς οἱ θεοὶ πάντες καὶ ἐν πρώτοις ὁ μέγας Σάραπις ἄρχειν ἐδικαίωσαν τῆς οἰκουμένης. Cf. 311 A. Serapis has his seat in Heaven as the brother of Zeus.

[3] 143 D. It may be noted that Proclus *in Tim.* 121 D calls the demiurgus πολυδύναμος.

[4] Julian even attempted to prove from Homer the superiority of Helios over the other gods. 136 D.

[5] 147 D.

[6] 149 B. So Romulus is the offspring of the Sun, as identified with Ares. 154 C.

[7] 144 A.

[8] 150 B. She is the σύγκρασις and φιλία of the οὐράνιοι θεοὶ and gives generative force to the earth. For Apollo as Asclepios see Julian, 144 D, C, and cf. Procl. *in Tim.* 49 C, where the similarity of language suggests that Julian here copied Iamblichus.

JULIAN'S RELATION TO PHILOSOPHY   59

Serapis, and the Egyptian Horus is Helios under another name.[1] Julian contrives that all the gods shall play their parts as manifestations of the power and beneficence of Helios.[2] In common with all who have called in philosophy to support their religious theories, Julian believed that a philosophic interpretation of myths was necessary for the genuine θεῶν γνῶσις. His treatment of them is ethical and metaphysical, and naturally has nothing in common with the rationalising method of Euhemerus.[3] Although, as we have seen, he explains his gods and demons as δυνάμεις, it must not be supposed that he intended, like the Stoics, to deprive them altogether of personality. The Stoic method was opposed to the spirit of Neoplatonism, and we find Plutarch protesting against their treatment of individual gods.

For Julian every myth is an allegory with a philosophic and instructive content which must be brought out by allegorical interpretation. It is an act of piety to free these hidden ideas and give them their true philosophic meaning. Plotinus had used the fables about the gods mainly as poetic ornament, but he too was far from regarding their allegorical interpretation as an intellectual game. They were invented by

[1] 148 D. Cf. Menander apud Spengel, *Rh. Gr.* iii.: Πέρσαι σε Μίθραν λέγουσιν Ὧρον Αἰγύπτιοι. So Julian identifies the Phrygian Cybele and the Greek Demeter, 159 ; Hermes and Ares with Monimos and Aziz, 150 ; the Phrygian Attis with Dionysus, 179.

[2] Julian is tolerant even of the God of the Jews, 454 A : ὃν εὖ οἶδ' ὅτι καὶ ἡμεῖς ἄλλοις θεραπεύομεν ὀνόμασιν.

[3] One instance of the Euhemeristic method occurs 220 D. Semele, says Julian, was not the mother of Dionysus, but was a wise priestess.

οἱ πάλαι σοφοί, in order that truths too sacred for direct expression might be disguised in riddles.[1] Plotinus attempted no systematic treatment of myths, though in several passages he indicates their metaphysical and ethical significance.[2] But Julian's aim was to account for the pagan deities in a system of religion and ethics, and his treatment of mythology is in consequence more elaborate, though he works on the same lines as Plotinus.

All the Sophists delighted in allegorising,[3] but whereas Themistius, Libanius, and, still more, Himerius, employed their allegories as literary ornament, Julian always allegorises with a didactic purpose. For him every myth was a riddle, and therefore to be solved. The poets who wrote the myths were inspired with the truth—εἶτα εὑρόντες ἐσκέπασαν αὐτὰ μύθοις παραδόξοις.[4] This very paradoxical element is intended to turn our minds to the hidden truths. For laymen the myth is enough: [5]—τοῖς δὲ περιττοῖς, the knowledge of divine things can only then be useful, εἴ τις ἐξετάζων αὐτὴν ὑφ' ἡγεμόσι τοῖς θεοῖς, εὕροι καὶ λάβοι διὰ τῶν αἰνιγμάτων ὑπομνησθεὶς

[1] *Ennead.* v. 1, 7: οἱ μῦθοι οἱ περὶ θεῶν αἰνίττονται Κρόνον μὲν θεὸν σοφώτατον πρὸ τοῦ Διὸς γενέσθαι, and *ib.* iii. 6, 19: οἱ πάλαι σοφοί . . . αἰνιττόμενοι, Ἑρμῆν μὲν ποιοῦσι τὸν ἀρχαῖον τὸ τῆς γενέσεως ὄργανον, and *ib.* i. 6, 8: οἷον ἀπὸ μάγου Κίρκης φησὶν ἢ Καλυψοῦς Ὀδυσσεὺς αἰνιττόμενος.

[2] *E.g.* The One is Οὐρανός; Κρόνος is Νοῦς; Ζεὺς the world-soul, &c. v. 8, 10; iii. 5, 3.

[3] Themist. 304 D, Hermog. *De Id.* p. 269, 18 sqq., Baumgart. *Aristides*, p. 63, Aphthon. *Progym.* p. 26, 10 sqq., Theo. *Prog.* p. 76, 5 sqq., ap. Spengel, *Rh. Graec.*

[4] 170 A, 222 C. The incongruous in a myth summons us to inquire into its underlying meaning. 136 C.

[5] 266 D. Myths are like india-rubber toys, which help children through teething.

ὅτι χρὴ περὶ αὐτῶν ζητεῖν.[1] A myth must aim at expressing the being of the divine.[2] The demon theory here played an important part. The lesser gods of Greek mythology are demons as well as δυνάμεις. Heracles was a good demon who after his work on earth became a god.[3] In his actual handling of details Julian sometimes uses the free method of interpretation that he had himself ridiculed in his second Oration.[4] And, like the other Neoplatonists, he sometimes employs phrases which imply human weaknesses or chronological development for his divinities, and then withdraws those phrases, explaining that they must be taken in a sense that denies such an interpretation. So the descent of Attis occurred οὐκ ἀκουσίως τοῖς θεοῖς, καὶ τῇ τούτων Μητρὶ, λεγομένη δὲ ἀκουσίως γενέσθαι.[5] Julian is always willing to abandon the details of a myth if they do not harmonise with his general conception.

Inseparable from his belief in the unity of religion

---

[1] Cf. Plat. *Theaet.* 152 C: τοῦτο ἡμῖν μὲν ἠνίξατο, τῷ πολλῷ συρφετῷ, τοῖς δὲ μαθηταῖς ἐν. ἀπορρητῷ τὴν ἀλήθειαν ἔλεγεν. Cf. Putarch's definition of a myth, *De I. et O.*: ὁ μῦθος.... λόγου τινὸς ἔμφασίς ἐστιν ἀνακλώντος ἐπ' ἄλλα τὴν διάνοιαν.

[2] 218 D: τῆς τῶν θεῶν οὐσίας εἰς δύναμιν ἐστοχασμένα.

[3] 219-20, cf. Plut. *De I. et O.* 27, for the same idea. Plutarch's treatment of myths often resembles Julian's, though it is not so metaphysical.

[4] 74 D: πόρρωθεν ἕλκοντες καὶ βιαζόμενοι τῶν ἔργων τὰς ὁμοιότητας, καθάπερ οἱ τοὺς μύθους ἐξηγούμενοι τῶν ποιητῶν καὶ ἀναλύοντες ἐς λόγους πιθανοὺς καὶ ἐνδεχομένους τὰ πλάσματα ἐκ μικρᾶς πάνυ τῆς ὑπονοίας ὁρμώμενοι καὶ ἀμυδρὰς λίαν παραλαβόντες τὰς ἀρχὰς πειρῶνται συμπείθειν ὡς δὴ ταῦτά γε αὐτὰ ἐκείνων ἐθελόντων λέγειν.

[5] 171 B: ἀγανακτεῖ μὲν οὐκέτι ἀγανακτοῦσα δὲ λέγεται, and 171 D: ἐκπεσὼν μὲν αὐτῶν οὐδαμῶς ἐκπεσεῖν δὲ λεγόμενος; and 149 B.

was Julian's theory of the unity of philosophy, a theory which, in an age of syncretism, was not peculiar to the Neoplatonists.[1] But it is in Julian's sixth Oration that we find its most systematic expression; and probably no other writer, except perhaps Iamblichus, had thought it so essential to his conceptions of Philosophy and Religion. Julian treated the question from the ethical side. As truth is one, so philosophy is one;[2] we may approach it by different roads,[3] but the τέλος of any one school, rightly interpreted, is found to be identical with the τέλος of any other.[4] The Cynic γνῶθι σεαυτὸν is but another reading of their παραχάραξον τὸ νόμισμα;[5] both, again, are in harmony with the Stoic ideal of life in touch with Nature—ὁμολογουμένως ζῆν τῇ φύσει,[6] and the Platonic ὁμοίωσις τῷ θεῷ.[7] So Pythagoras, Socrates, Plato, Aristotle, Zeno, and Antisthenes followed ἕν τι καὶ ταὐτόν.[8]

Julian excepted Epicurus and Pyrrho from this general reconciliation; and this was natural. He would not admit that their τέλος was ethical; and the universal scepticism of the Pyrrhonists and the Epicurean rejection of the supernatural were alike

[1] Cf. footnote on Themistius and Eugenius *supra*, p. 38.
[2] 184 c.
[3] 185 A.
[4] 183 A.
[5] For, ὁ γνοὺς ἑαυτὸν, ὅπερ ἔστιν, ἀκριβῶς εἴσεται καὶ οὐχ ὅπερ νομίζεται, 183 B.
[6] 186 A.
[7] 183 A.
[8] 188 c, cf. 185 A: τοὺς πρωτεύσαντας ἐν ἑκάστῃ τῶν αἱρέσεων σκοπείτω (τις) καὶ εὑρήσει πάντα σύμφωνα. For the harmony of Stoic and Peripatetic doctrines, see Julian, *Ep.* 17, 386.

incompatible with the uncritical faith that he was trying to restore.¹ His aim throughout his ὕμνοι was to provide the Hellenic counterpart of the positive revealed religion of Christianity. Hence his insistence on the inspiration of Homer, Hesiod, and Plato. And we can trace to this effort the statement that the allegorical interpretations of the mysteries are not mere hypotheses, whereas the doctrines of the astronomers of the day deserve no higher title.² Julian rejected the Epicureans and Sceptics mainly on the score of their critical attitude to religion. The Cynics were, from the first, Deists, who scoffed at polytheism, image-worship, and oracles. All Julian's sophistry could not explain away the independent monotheism of Diogenes;³ Antisthenes laughed at initiation; Demonax nearly brought upon himself the

¹ Julian naturally could not admit an αὐτόματος φορὰ καὶ τύχη, 162 A. Themistius, in his desire for syncretism, was more liberal, and even criticises his father Eugenius for having omitted Epicurus from the κατάλογος of philosophers, 236 A. Elsewhere, however, he is less friendly to Epicurean doctrines, e.g. Or. 34. 74. Even Julian defends the Epicurean λαθὲ βιώσας, 255 B.

² 423 A, 149 c, 136 B, 137 c et passim, cf. Macrob. Sat. i. 17, 2: cave aestimes poetarum gregem non ab adytis philosophiae mutuari. οἱ μὲν γὰρ (the philosophers) θεῶν ἢ δαιμόνων μεγάλων δή τινων ἀκούσαντές φασιν, οἱ δὲ (the astronomers) ὑποτίθενται τὸ πιθανὸν ἐκ τῆς πρὸς τὰ φαινόμενα συμφωνίας, 148 B. That a preference for theurgy over mathematics was characteristic of the Neoplatonists, we may gather from a comparison of Proclus, in Tim. 258 c: ἀλλὰ τῶν μὲν μαθηματικῶν οὐ πολὺς λόγος πιθανολογούντων· ὁ δὲ θεουργὸς οὕτως οἴεται κ.τ.λ. It is true that in this case Proclus is merely accepting the Platonic rejection of mathematical πιθανολογία as distinct from mathematics generally; cf. Aristot. Ethics, i. 3, 4 : μαθηματικοῦ ... πιθανολογοῦντος, which is an echo of Plat. Theaet. 162 E.

³ Or. vi. 199 et al.

fate of Socrates, ὅτι οὔτε θύων ὤφθη πώποτε οὔτε ἐμυήθη μόνος ἁπάντων ταῖς Ἐλευσινίαις.[1] Oenomaus of Gadara wrote a work against oracles.[2] Yet Julian not only accepted the Cynic τέλος, but expressly declared that Cynicism was worthy to rank with the highest philosophy.[3] There is more than one explanation of this inconsistency. The Cynic ascesis, and the life κατὰ φύσιν, as interpreted by Diogenes and Antisthenes, appealed strongly to his personal tastes.[4] But apart from this, the canonisation of Diogenes had become a literary tradition, and if Julian had refused his tribute of admiration, he would have found himself in sympathy with only one writer of distinction—the scoffer Lucian.[5] This would have been a singularly false position for Julian; for one of the grounds of Lucian's scorn of the Cynics had been their belief in a divinity, his only bond of sympathy with them their ridicule of polytheism. Julian shared the sincere admiration which the Cynic ideal of life had won from such men as Epictetus,[6]

[1] Lucian, *Demonax*, 11.
[2] Julian, 209 B.
[3] 182 C: ἐπειδὴ τὸν κυνισμὸν εἶδός τι φιλοσοφίας εἶναι συμβέβηκεν, οὔ τι φαυλότατον οὐδὲ ἀτιμότατον, ἀλλὰ τοῖς κρατίστοις ἐνάμιλλον κ.τ.λ. Apollo, not Heracles, is the true patron of Cynicism, 188.
[4] The ignorant crowd had always laughed at the Cynic ἄσκησις, and there Julian sympathised with the Cynics, 198 A: τῶν Κυνικῶν εἴ πού τις γέγονε σπουδαῖος, ἐλεεινὸς δοκεῖ.
[5] Bernays, *Lucian und die Cyniker*, pp. 46 sqq., has explained Lucian's antagonism to the Cynic sect. For his attitude to Diogenes see *Vit. Auct.* 11.
[6] Epictetus recognised the divine mission of the true Cynic: τὸν ταῖς ἀληθείαις Κυνικὸν εἰδέναι δεῖ, ὅτι ἄγγελος ἀπὸ τοῦ Διὸς ἀπέσταλται πρὸς τοὺς ἀνθρώπους περὶ ἀγαθῶν καὶ κακῶν ὑποδείξων αὐτοῖς ὅτι πεπλάνηται κ.τ.λ., *Diss.* iii. 22. 23.

Dio Chrysostomus, and Maximus of Tyre.¹ But, like them, he had nothing but invective for the Cynics who were his contemporaries. These Cynics of the fourth century, who, with their mode of living, had survived the abstract theories and systems of most of the other schools,² seem to have still held, by profession, to their founder's conception of life. In the confused times in which Julian lived, there can have been few types that had changed so little, outwardly, from their originals as the Cynic.³ There was little room for change in the members of a school whose philosophy was wholly negative—meant as a protest against the artificial world around it, whatever the phase in which that world might happen to be. It is the brawling Alcidamas of Lucian,⁴ or Plutarch's Planetiades,⁵ and not the dignified and witty Demonax, who typifies the later Cynic.⁶ The reasons for Julian's dislike of practical fourth century Cynicism lie close at hand. They were bad citizens with their

[1] His thirty-sixth Dissertation is a panegyric of Diogenes. Epictetus, *Diss.* iii. 22, 80: ἀλλ' εἰς τοὺς νῦν ἀποβλέπομεν τοὺς τραπεζῆας, πυλαωροὺς, οἳ οὐδὲν μιμοῦνται ἐκείνους; cf. Julian, 197 B, and for the ideal Cynic cf. Epictetus, iii. 22, 13, with Julian, 200 C, D.

[2] S. Aug. *Con. Acad.* iii. 19, 42: Nunc philosophos non fere videmus nisi aut Cynicos aut Peripateticos aut Platonicos; et Cynicos quidem quia eos vitae quaedam delectat libertas atque licentia.

[3] βακτηρία, τρίβων, κόμη, τὸ ἐντεῦθεν ἀμαθία, θράσος, ἰταμότης καὶ πάντα ἁπλῶς τὰ τοιαῦτα, Julian, 225.

[4] Lucian, *Lapithae*.

[5] Plut. *De Def. Orac.* 7, 413.

[6] Some of them wished, like Oenomaus and Heraclius, against whom Julian's sixth Oration is directed, to shake off the authority of Diogenes. Cf. J. 180, 181: ἀνὴρ Κυνικὸς Διογένη φησὶ κενόδοξον, and 236 B: πρὸς τοὺς κρατίστους τῶν Κυνικῶν εἴ τις ἄρα ἔστι νῦν τοιοῦτος κ.τ.λ.

F

negative cosmopolitanism;[1] they set an example of laziness and immorality; their illiteracy was offensive to Julian as a man of letters.[2] But it was the discredit they brought on philosophy in general,[3] and their ridicule of the religion that he was trying to revive, which roused Julian to write his two orations against them. Their resemblance to the Christians, which had been pointed out by Aristides,[4] naturally did not recommend them to Julian.

[1] J. 224 B: καταλελοίπατε τὴν πατρίδα ὥσπερ ἐκεῖνοι (οἱ Γαλιλαῖοι).
[2] 227 A. 203 B: εἰ σμικρὰ τὰς βίβλους ἀνελίττων ἐμελέτας ... ἔγνως ἂν ... ἀλλ' οὐκ ἔστι σοι τούτων οὐδὲν κ.τ.λ.; and cf. 237 A. For Cynicism as a refuge for those who had failed in other professions, cf. Luc. Δραπέται and Peregrinus the ex-Christian. All who aimed at τὸ περιβλέπεσθαι, says Julian, find their opportunity in Cynicism, 225 B: τῶν ῥητορικῶν οἱ δυσμαθέστατοι ... ὁρμῶσιν ἐπὶ τὸν Κυνισμόν.
[3] 223 D: πρὸς τῶν ἀκροωμένων οἳ δι' ὑμᾶς τὴν φιλοσοφίαν ἐκτρέπονται. Cf. Aristid. vol. ii. p. 401: ἀφεστᾶσι τῶν Ἑλλήνων. Cf. Julian, 225 A.
[4] Vol. ii. p. 402 D: τοῖς ἐν Παλαιστίνῃ δυσσεβέσι παραπλήσιοι τοὺς τρόπους. Cf. Julian, 224 c; ἴσως δὲ καὶ διὰ τὸ μηδὲν ὑμῶν εἶναι πρόσχημα τοῦ φορολογεῖν εὐπροσώπως ὁποῖον ἐκείνοις, ἣν λέγουσιν οὐκ οἶδ' ὅπως ἐλεημοσύνην, τὰ δ' ἄλλα γε πάντα ἐστὶν ὑμῖν τε κἀκείνοις παραπλήσια. καταλελοίπατε τὴν πατρίδα ὥσπερ ἐκεῖνοι, περιφοιτᾶτε πάντῃ κ.τ.λ. For cases of Cynics becoming Christians, see Bernays, op. cit. note 21.

CHAPTER III

JULIAN'S STYLE AND VOCABULARY

A CRITIC of Julian's style is at first inclined to recognise two distinct classes in his works, and to separate those that may be regarded as the fruit of a careful study of Rhetoric, or were, at any rate, composed in comparative leisure, from those that are obviously, as well as professedly, autoschediastic. To the first class would naturally belong *Orr.* i.–iii.; viii.; *Ep. ad Themistium*; *Ep. ad Ath.*; *Frag. Ep.*; *Caesars*; *Misopogon*. In the second class one would place *Orr.* iv. v.[1] vi.[2] vii., and most of the Letters.

Yet, even in the panegyrics, which, as has been indicated,[3] betray a technical knowledge of epideictic oratory, we frequently find the excuse of the layman,[4] and the effort to disarm the criticism of οἱ λίαν σοφοὶ and οἱ κομψοὶ ῥήτορες (77 A) is natural enough in a man who had sufficient taste and training to know how far his own compositions fell short of his models. The stock excuse of haste,[5] or lack of professional

---

[1] 178 D: *Or.* v. was written in one night, without preparation; *Or.* iv. in three nights, 157 c.
[2] 203 c: πάρεργον ἡμέραιν δυοῖν; cf. 216 A.
[3] See *supra*, analysis of *Or.* i.
[4] *E.g.* 2 A, 3 c, 2 D, 120, 125 A, 126 B, 105 A.
[5] We learn from Isocrates, *Or.* 412, that it was a commonplace in

ease in writing, has more significance than usual in the mouth of a soldier and statesman, who had to snatch from the business of the court or the camp his opportunites for literary composition. And it is seldom absent from Julian's works.[1] If he does but compose a letter he protests that the style of a man of affairs must not be judged by the rhetorician's standards.[2]

All his work, even when not autoschediastic, shows here and there a lack of the file, as will be indicated later. He is singularly free from anacolutha,[3] and his frequent parentheses are usually short, and rarely confuse the narrative. His style in narrating, as seen in the historical parts of the panegyrics, is simple and straightforward.[4] In the *Misopogon* and the *Caesars* it is concise and often dramatic. His philosophical writing, however, is darkened by the obscurity that came of the effort to make a clear statement of arguments which he had had no time to arrange, and of

a rhetorical prooemium to plead ὡς ἐξ αὐτογνίου γέγονεν ἡ παρασκευή.

[1] *Or*. ii. was written in Gaul, 56 B, 101 D: ἐμοί τε οὐ σχολὴ τὰς μούσας ἐπὶ τοσοῦτον θεραπεύειν, ἀλλ' ὥρα λοιπὸν πρὸς ἔργον τρέπεσθαι; cf. 8 c, 105 A.

[2] 374 A, D, 428 B: εἴ τι ἡμάρτηται μὴ πικρῶς ἐξέταζε μηδ' ὡς ῥήτωρ ῥήτορα.

[3] 19 c: ὁ δὲ ὑπὲρ τῆς ἀρχῆς ... δοκῶν βεβουλεῦσθαι ... πόσων ἐπαίνων ἄξιον κρινεῖ τις; 200 B: ἐντυχὼν ... οὐδὲν δεήσει τὸν ἄνδρα; 329 B: πρὸς ἐκείνην βλέπων οὐδὲν ἔμελεν αὐτῷ; ... 30 c: ὁπόσοις εἰρήνης μέλει καὶ τὴν ὁμόνοιαν ἐκ παντὸς στέργουσιν; 23 c: ἐκπληττόμενοι ... οἱ πολέμιοι ... ἤρχετο μὲν οὐδείς. Cf. 167 D, 239 B.

[4] Such curious arrangements as 36 B: διαλυθείσης δὲ, οἱ στρατιῶται, τῆς τάξεως, and 32 D: οἱ δειλοί, τῶν πολεμίων ἐν ὕψει, στρατηγοί, are infrequent, but Cobet (in *Mnemosyne*, x. 433) in suggesting the transposition of the words of the last passage seems to make hardly enough allowance for the affectation of the period.

theories which he himself only vaguely realised. Thus he labours to be coherent, and by force of repetition becomes confused.[1] Sometimes the tautology is so glaring that we must suppose it to have been involuntary.[2] It occurs most frequently in the philosophical works, which were hastily written and never revised. But it is so conspicuous in the more studied orations that we are justified in regarding clumsy repetition as a characteristic of Julian's style.[3]

Ammianus records that he was a great talker: *linguae fusioris et admodum raro silentis*;[4] his loquacity is reflected in his writings. The use of synonyms was a rhetorical device to give fulness (περιβολή);[5] Julian carries it to excess.[6] He is fond of digressions,

---

[1] Instances of this are *Or.* iv. 140 c, D: εἰ τὴν ἐν τοῖς νοητοῖς ἄχραντον καὶ καθαρὸν ἄυλον οὐσίαν νοήσαιμεν . . . πλήρη τῆς οἰκείας ἀχράντου καθαρότητος, τήν τε ἐν τῷ κόσμῳ λίαν εἰλικρινῆ καὶ καθαρὰν φύσιν ἀχράντου σώματος εὑρήσομεν καὶ τὴν τοῦ Ἡλίου λαμπρὰν καὶ ἀκήρατον οὐσίαν ἀμφοῖν μέσην, τῆς τε ἐν τοῖς νοητοῖς ἀύλου καθαρότητος καὶ τῆς ἐν τοῖς αἰσθητοῖς ἀχράντου καὶ ἀμιγοῦς πρὸς γένεσιν καὶ φθορὰν καθαρᾶς εἰλικρινείας.

[2] 144 B, c and 166 D with 167 A; 185 c with 186 A and 231 A: ὦ Ζεῦ πάτερ ἢ ὅ τι σοι φίλον ὄνομα καὶ ὅπως ὀνομάζεσθαι; 132 A: τὸ κεφάλαιον . . . τῆς ἀνθρωπίνης ἐν τῷ δύνασθαι φράζειν δυνάμεως; 249 A: he heaps up three equivalent proverbs to express one simple idea; 64 A: ἐξαναβῶμεν αὖθις εἰς ἴχνος καὶ ὅθεν ἐξέβην.

[3] 21 c, D: κατέστησας . . . καταστησάμενος . . . κατέστησας . . . κατέστησας. Here Reiske would omit the last; but cf. 17 A: καταστησάμενος twice; 153 A: καταστησαμένοις twice; 30 B: προσκαθημένος —προσκαθημένα; 42 D–43 A: πάλαι στερομένοις . . . στερομένοις πάλαι; 152 B, c: κατενοήσαμεν twice; which seem to put emendation out of the question; 26 A is peculiarly awkward: χρὴ . . . λογίζεσθαι . . . τὸ δὲ ὑπολαβεῖν . . . τὸ δὲ λογίζεσθαι.

[4] Ammian. xv. 4.

[5] Hermog. *de Id.* p. 321.

[6] *E.g.* 49 E: ψαλτήριον ἁρμοσάμενον καὶ κιθάραν ᾄδειν καὶ ὑμνεῖν; 339 D: ὥσπερ τινὰ φόρον ἢ δασμὸν εἰσφέρων καὶ ἀποδιδούς. Such

and usually indicates his return to the subject by a ὅθεν δ' ἐξέβην,[1] a favourite phrase with the fourth-century rhetoricians, who constantly wander into Platonic digressions[2] and illustrations from Greek literature.

It was from them that Julian caught his trick of harping on a classic phrase or metaphor. Thucydides, or Sophocles, or Plato may have used such a phrase once; Julian will repeat it half-a-dozen times. Plato and Sophocles had each once used the verb ἐντήκειν to express the depth of an emotion.[3] Julian imitates them five times.

He wrote the reminiscence Greek of the revived literature, and every page of his writings is full of echoes of the Greek masterpieces, the close study of which, for the purposes of oratory, was indispensable to a Sophist's training.[4] Julian often cites passages with the author's name, but his more usual method is to weave into his prose half-verses, phrases, and even

---

collocations as ἰῷτο καὶ θεραπεύοι, θωπεῦσαι καὶ κολακεῦσαι, χαίρων καὶ γεγηθώς, must strike the most casual reader of Julian by their frequency; a good instance is 317 D: ἦν τὸ σῶμα διαυγέστατον καὶ διαφανέστατον ὥσπερ τὸ καθαρώτατον καὶ εἰλικρινέστατον φῶς.

[1] 288 c, 59 c, 64 A, 69 D, 92 D, 190 A, 200 B, 226 D, 266 C.

[2] Julian apologises for the frequency of his own digressions into philosophy, 69 D.

[3] Soph. *El.* 1311, Pl. *Menex.* 245; cf. Julian, 130 c, 226 A, 251 D, 206 B, 378 A. So, too, Aristides, p. 417 D. It may be noted that, while Julian uses μόγις καὶ ἀγαπητῶς five times (345, 273, 369, 142, 276), in Aelian and Aristides it occurs only once. So Themistius and Libanius worked into almost every oration the sentence ἀσκεῖται τὸ τιμώμενον (*Rep.* 551 A).

[4] Cf. Liban. *Or.* 65, p. 438. His pupils question the advantage of their rhetorical studies, 'for which they have to read so much poetry.'

whole sentences without any such acknowledgment. His use of Homeric quotations is an exception to this rule. While, in the majority of cases, he weaves in, or slightly alters his reminiscences of Plato or Euripides, he usually indicates, either directly or indirectly, the source of Homeric phrases or verses.[1] The reason for this may have been that while he had no hesitation in using an Attic phrase, however poetical, he felt that Epic diction was out of place in prose.[2] Julian quotes Homer more frequently than any other author. Among prose writers Plato is naturally his favourite. His Neoplatonism would have accounted for this. But, apart from that, he was merely following the example of all the writers of late Greek prose, whether Neoplatonists or not. Even Aristides, who took Demosthenes for his model, has more than twice as many purely Platonic as purely Demosthenic words in his vocabulary; and what is true of Aristides is still more true of Themistius and Libanius.

The direct reminiscences in Julian will be discussed later. But, even supposing them to be a complete collection, they by no means represent the influence of Plato on Julian's language. It is from the half-phrases and subtle allusions[3] that occur on

---

[1] Out of 135 Homeric quotations less than a dozen are without such acknowledgment.

[2] The following are instances of Epic phrases worked in without indication of their origin:—χήτει τοῦ χαλινοῦ, 50 B; ἴσον θυμὸν ἔχοντες, 241; ᾤχετο ἄϊστος ἄφαντος, 59; ἐντεῦθεν ἐλόντες, 123, 229; κουρίδιον ἄνδρα, 110; ἐκ τῶν οἷοι νῦν βροτοί εἰσιν, 248; νεῶν ἔρματα, 27; ὀλλύντων καὶ ὀλλυμένων, 27 (cf. Il. 4. 450); ἐγνωκὼς τὸ πλησίον ὄρος ἀμφικαλύψαι τῇ πόλει, 28; βοῶν ἀγέλη, 37; ὥσπερ πατὴρ ἤπιος, 345; Πατρόκλῳ ἐπίηρα φέρων, 351; οὐδ' ἂν ἡβῶν ἀνήρ, 118 A (Il. 12. 382).

[3] A few of these may be given for the sake of illustration:—145,

every page that we feel the extent of Julian's familiarity with his author.

In his free use of poetic diction, Julian again follows the tradition of the prose writers of the post-classical period. Poetry had been for centuries in the shade of Rhetoric (Rohde, *Griech. Roman*, p. 332), and poetical composition seems to have been out of fashion in Julian's day.[1] But the use of whole verses and of poetic phrases and words was always recognised by the Sophists as an effective means of giving γλυκύτης[2] to their prose, and it became more and more popular, in spite of the efforts of the rigid Atheists,[3] until it reached its climax in the prose poetry of Himerius. In Julian's genuine writings

γεννᾶν ἐν τῷ καλῷ ; 148 C, ὥσπερ τὰ βοσκήματα θεωροῦντες (*Rep*. 586 A, βοσκημάτων δίκην βλέπειν) ; 70 B, γήινον σῶμα (*Phaedr*. 246 c); 308 A, νῷ θεατόν ; 350 C, πόλις ἤδη τρυφῶσα (*Rep*. 372) ; 23 B, 26 A, πνίγους ῥώμη (*Laws* 633 c); 42 B, αὐτὸ τὸ καλόν ; 25 C, ἐν ὁμαλῷ καὶ λείῳ (*Tim*. 34 B) ; 82 B, χρόνῳ πολιόν ; 124 B, πολιὸν τὸν νοῦν (*Tim*. μάθημα πολιὸν χρόνῳ) ; 197 B, πολυκέφαλον θηρίον (*Rep*.); 297, θεῶν κτῆμα (*Phaed*.) ; 248 B, ὅσοις ἀξίως βεβίωται τῆς τοιαύτης θέας ; 85 B, ἀνάγκη πεινῆν διὰ βίου (*Laws*, 832 A).

[1] *Misop*. 337 B : ἀφαιρεῖται δὲ τὴν ἐν τοῖς μέλεσι μουσικὴν ὁ νῦν ἐπικρατῶν ἐν τοῖς ἐλευθέροις τῆς παιδείας τρόπος. αἴσχιον γὰρ εἶναι δοκεῖ νῦν μουσικὴν ἐπιτηδεύειν ἢ πάλαι ποτὲ ἐδόκει τὸ πλουτεῖν ἀδίκως ; cf. Liban. *Ep*. 1113, Themist. 347 B : τὰ σμικρὰ ταῦτα καὶ χαμαίζηλα (of poetry).

[2] Hermog. *De Id*. p. 362. 10 Sp.

[3] Schmid, *Att*. i. p. 208. Dion. Hal. praised Lysias for abstaining from poetic diction (*De Lys*. 3), and censured Plato for using it (*Ad Pomp*. 2). The following are among the more noteworthy phrases worked into Julian's prose :—43 B, ἐν δίκῃ καὶ παρὰ δίκην (Pind.) ; cf. 114 C, 227 D ; 370 A, λιμὸν ἀλοιητῆρα βρότειον ; 383 D, ῥῖψον ἢ ποταμῷ κλῦσον ; 255 A, τὸ σῶμα τῇ μητρὶ γῇ δοῦναι ; 97 A, ποθεινὸς τοῖς φίλοις ; 109 D, γαμήλιον ἀνάψαι λαμπάδα ; 217 C, ἕπεται ὕβρις κόρῳ ; 25 C, νεὼς ἰθυντήρ—ἅρματος ἐπιστάτης : 211 B, γῆν πρὸ γῆς (Æsch. ; Aristoph.).

there is no approach to the lyrical style of Himerius.[1] His poetic vocabulary shows a wide range of reading, but in measuring the influence on his style of his study of the poets we have to note some curious omissions. It is perhaps significant of the taste of his age in poetry that, while there are many reminiscences of Euripides in Julian, there are none of Aeschylus, and very few of Sophocles or Pindar. Even his references to Euripides are confined to four plays, and, with the exception of Homer, a close knowledge of whom may be taken for granted in an educated Greek of any period, Julian concerned himself far more with prose, especially the prose of Plato and Aristotle. His neglect of the lyric poets is conspicuous. His use of special authors may be tested by the following statistics.[2]

According to Schwarz, Julian's quotations of Homer[3] number Iliad (82), Odyssey (53), Hesiod (7), Theognis (1), Sappho (4), Anacreon (2), Simonides (3), Pindar (7),[4] Sophocles (4), Euripides (16), Melanthius (1), Epicharmus (1), Eupolis (1), Aristo-

---

[1] Cf. Him. *Or.* i. 2 and xiv. 10, and πε.θὼ δὲ καὶ πόθοι κ.τ.λ. in *Or.* i. 19, for specimens of his florid poetical diction.

[2] The following figures are drawn from an article by Schwarz (*Philologus*, vol. 51. 4. 1892. 'Julianstudien'), and the reader is referred to it for the exact references. The collection of reminiscences there given was based on the indications given by Hertlein in the critical notes to the Teubner edition, though a few additions were made. But the collection was by no means complete, as the additions given below will show.

[3] It should be observed that Schwarz has collected from the Letters to Iamblichus and from the Letters rejected by Hertlein, while I have not taken into consideration here, or at all in this chapter, the letters above mentioned (see *Appendix* i.).

[4] Add Julian 290 B quotes Pindar, *Ol.* 7. 49 (noted by Hertlein).

phanes (6), Philemon (1), Menander (1), Herodotos (5), Xenophon (3), Demosthenes (8), Heraclitus (5), Empedocles (1), Plato (51), Aristotle (16), Hippocrates (2), Theocritus (3), Callimachus (1), Crates (2), Babrius (2).

To these I would add the following, arranging authors in the order observed by Schwarz :—

Iliad ix. 380 and 401: οὐ γὰρ ἐμοὶ ψυχῆς ἀντάξιον κ.τ.λ.
J. 120 D : οὐ τὸν ἐπὶ γῆς .... ἀντάξιον κ.τ.λ.

EURIPIDES.
Androm. 368.
J. 97 A : οὔτι φαυλότερον ἔργον ἢ Τροίαν ἑλεῖν.[1]

Phoen. 551.   J. 200 C.
Phoen. 517.   J. 73 C.
Hipp. 183.   J. 250 D : ὑπερορῶν ἀεὶ τῶν παρόντων κ.τ.λ.[2]

EUPOLIS.
Δημ. 6.
J. 33 A and 426 B : πειθὼ τοῖς χείλεσιν κ.τ.λ.

XENOPHON.
de Rep. Lac. 15, 7.   J. 14 D.
Anab. 7, 1, 29.   J. 198 C : μυρίας ὀργυιὰς κατὰ γῆς.

DEMOSTHENES.
Or. xviii. 18.
J. 33 C : πόλεμος .... ὁποῖον τὸν Φωκικὸν ἀκούομεν συστῆναι (Pet.).[3]

---

[1] This is rather a proverb than a direct reminiscence, though Hertlein has not included it in his collection of proverbs in Index.

[2] This seems better than to refer it to Democr. *frag.* 31.

[3] A famous locus; cf. *Rhet. Graec.* (Spengel), ii. p. 324, 2; 329, 3; iii. 20, 26; 139, 20.

JULIAN'S STYLE AND VOCABULARY 75

DEMOSTHENES—*continued*.

Or. xviii. 23.
J. 267 A: βοῶ καὶ μαρτύρομαι.

Or. xviii. 47, 52.
J. 203 C: ἀλλ' οὐκ ἔστι.... πόθεν; πολλοῦ γε καὶ δεῖ.[1]

Or. xviii. 61.
J. 26 C: τυράννων φοράν.[2]

Or. xviii. 59 : ἀπαρτᾶν τὸν λόγον τῆς γραφῆς.
J. 64 A: ἀπαρτᾶν τὸν λόγον καὶ ἀποπλανᾶσθαι τῆς ὑποθέσεως.[3]

Or. xviii. 153 : ὥσπερ χειμάρρους κ.τ.λ.
J. 29 D, 34 C.

Or. xviii. 169 : ἑσπέρα μὲν γὰρ ἦν .... κατείληπται.
J. 26 B: ἦν μὲν γὰρ ὁ χειμών... ἦκε δὲ ἀγγέλλων τις... κατείληπται.[4]

Or. xx. 461, 15 : τῇ δὲ τιμῇ .... δωρεάς.
J. 44 B, C.

Or. xxi. 153.
J. 364 D: ἀηδίας .... ἀποκναῖσαι.

Or. xxv. 52 : πορεύεται ἠρκὼς τὸ κέντρον.
J. 99 B: διηρμένων .... τὰ κέντρα.[5]

PLATO.

Phaed. 83 D : λύπη ... τὸ σῶμα.
J. 136 B : λυθείσας αὐτὰς (ψυχάς) σώμασιν ἑτέροις προσηλοῖ.

[1] καὶ μὴν αἱ ἐπικρίσεις τοιαῦται, οἷον, πόθεν; πολλοῦ κ.τ.λ. R. G. (Spengel), ii. 382, 32.
[2] Theon, ap. Spengel, ii. 68, 1.
[3] An instance of Julian's love of amplification.
[4] A favourite passage with the rhetoricians ; *Auct.* περὶ ὕψους *ch.* 10; Spengel, ii. 346, 17 ; 349, 20 ; 326, 23 ; iii. 140, 7 ; ii. p. 70.
[5] Hence Cobet prefers to read here the uncompounded verb.

PLATO—continued.

Phaed. 63 c.	J. 212 B: οἷα πρὸς ἀγαθοὺς δεσπότας (τοὺς θεούς).
Phaed. 62 B.	J. 276 B: εἴ τι τῶν σῶν κτημάτων ἀποστεροίη σε κ.τ.λ.
Republic, 577 E.	J. 50 c: χρὴ τοὺς μὲν βασιλέας .... ἵνα μὴ μεταμελείας αὐτοῖς ὁ βίος μεστὸς ᾖ.
Republic, 354 B.	J. 69 c: ὥσπερ .... οἱ λίχνοι κ.τ.λ.
Republic, 493 A.	J. 78 c, D is an echo of the passage.
Republic, 416: τὰ δὲ ἐπιτήδεια .... ὅσον μήτε περιεῖναι — μήτε ἐνδεῖν κ.τ.λ.	J. 92 A: οὔτε αὐθαδὲς .... οὔτε μὴν ἐνδεὲς τῶν ἀναγκαίων κ.τ.λ., cf. J. 86 D-87 A for an echo of the simile of the bad shepherd.
Republic, 382 D.	J. 221 D: διὰ τὸ ἀγνοεῖν ἔτι περὶ αὐτῶν τὸ ἀκριβές ....
Republic, 377: On myths .... ἐγκριτέον ... and tone of passage.	J. 219 A: On myths ... ἐγκριτέον .... and tone of passage.
Republic, 618 B: ἔνθα δὴ .... ὁ πᾶς κίνδυνος.	J. 230 D: ἐνταῦθά ἐστιν ὁ μέγας κίνδυνος.
Republic, 489 A: ἄχρηστοι τοῖς πολλοῖς οἱ ἐπιεικέστατοι τῶν ἐν φιλοσοφίᾳ.	J. 410 c: τὸ δοκεῖν ἀχρήστους εἶναι ταῖς πόλεσι τοὺς μετιόντας φιλοσοφίαν.

PLATO—*continued*.

Republic, 563 C: τὸ μὲν γὰρ τῶν θηρίων .... ὅσῳ ἐλευθερώτερά ἐστιν ἐνταῦθα .... γίγνονταί γε δὴ καὶ ἵπποι καὶ ὄνοι πάνυ ἐλευθέρως .... εἰθισμένοι πορεύεσθαι κατὰ τὰς ὁδούς κ.τ.λ.

Republic, 519 A.

Laws, 937 D.

Laws, 714 A.

Laws, 730 D.

J. 355 B: τὸ γὰρ τῆς πόλεως ἦθος .... ἐλεύθερον λίαν .... οὐδ' ἀποβλέψας ὅση καὶ μέχρι τῶν ὄνων ἐστὶν ἐλευθερία .... αἱ πλατεῖαι τῶν ὁδῶν οὐκ ἐπὶ τούτῳ .... χρῆσθαι δὲ ὑπ' ἐλευθερίας οἱ ὄνοι βούλονται ταῖς στοαῖς κ.τ.λ.

J. 161 B: τοῖς κομψοῖς ὧν τὸ ψυχάριον δριμὺ μὲν ὑγιὲς δέ κ.τ.λ.

J. 91 A: τὰς δὲ οἷον κῆρας .... ἐκφεύγων; and 262 D: οὐ ῥᾴδιον .... ἐκφυγεῖν κῆρας ....[1]

J. 182 C: τὴν τοῦ νοῦ διανομὴν, cf. infra 258-59 where the passage from the Laws, including these words, is quoted at length.

J. 316 C: ὅρα .... μή ποτε οὗτοι ἑνὸς ὦσιν ἀντάξιοι τουτονὶ .... cf. infra 353 D, where Julian quotes the passage from the Laws.

[1] Cf. too D. Hal. *A. R.* 2. 3: προσεῖναι δέ τινας ἑκάστῃ (τῶν πολιτειῶν) κῆρας ... and *ib.* 8. 61: ὁ δαίμων , .. ἑτέρας οὐκ εὐτυχεῖς κῆρας ... προσῆψε.

PLATO—continued.

Laws, 917 B.	J. 208 B : χραίνειν οὐκ εὐαγῶς τὴν ἐπωνυμίαν τοῦ βασιλέως Ἡλίου.
Laws, 676 A.	J. 148 B : καὶ ταῦτα μὲν δὴ ταύτῃ, φασί.[1]
Theaetetus, 175 D.	J. 57 A.
Theaetetus, 176 A.	J. 90 A : τὰ κακὰ δὲ οὔτ' ἐγέννησεν κ.τ.λ.
Theaetetus, 161 A and 151 E.	J. 206 C : ὑπηνέμια καὶ τερατώδη .... ἐπιστήμης οἷον εἴδωλα.
Timaeus, 41 A, B.	J. 132 C.
Timaeus, 42 D : ἔσπειρε τοὺς μὲν εἰς γῆν.	J. 131 C.
Timaeus, 58 A.	J. 139 C : ἡ πάντα .... σφίγγει.
Timaeus, 32 D : ὅλον .... ζῷον τέλεον ἐκ τελέων.	J. 139 B : ζῷον ὅλον .... τέλειον ἐκ μερῶν τελείων.
Timaeus, 77 B : πᾶν γὰρ .... ζῷον .... ἂν .... λέγοιτο.	J. 193 B : ἡ Πλατωνικὴ ... δόξα ἔμψυχα ὑπολαμβάνουσα καὶ τὰ φύτα.
Timaeus, 41 A : πάντες ὅσοι περιπολοῦσιν.	J. 140 A : πολλοὶ δὲ οἱ κατ' οὐρανὸν περιπολοῦντες .... θεοί.
Timaeus, 32 B : πυρός τε καὶ γῆς κ.τ.λ.	J. 143 C.
Timaeus, 90 A.	J. 69 A : δαίμονα θεὸς ἑκάστῳ δέδωκε κ.τ.λ.

[1] Cobet points out (*Mnemos.* xi. p. 353) that though the phrase had become proverbial it goes back to Plato ; cf. Plut. *Demosth.* c. 4 : καὶ ταῦτα μὲν ταύτῃ, κατὰ Πλάτωνα.

JULIAN'S STYLE AND VOCABULARY

PLATO—*continued.*
Timaeus, 54 A.
Symposium, 174 B, D: ἄκλητος ἥκειν ἀλλά.... κεκλημένος.
Phaedrus, 247 B.

Phaedrus, 267 A: τά τε αὖ σμικρὰ μεγάλα καὶ τὰ μεγάλα σμικρὰ φαίνεσθαι ποιοῦσι.
Phaedrus, 251 C.
Epist. ii. 312 E: περὶ τὸν πάντων βασιλέα πάντ' ἐστί.

J. 216 B.
J. 201 B: Crates ἐπορεύετο ἐπὶ.... ἑστίας ἄκλητος κεκλημένος.[1]
J. 149 D: ἀπ' ἄκρας ἁψῖδος οὐρανοῦ.
J. 2 C.[2]

J. 206 D.
J. 132 C: διὰ τὸν πάντων βασιλέα, περὶ ὃν πάντα ἐστίν.[3]

ARISTOTLE.
Ethics, iv. 2, 1: δοκεῖ γὰρ καὶ αὐτὴ περὶ χρήματά τις ἀρετὴ εἶναι....

J. 129 D: καί τοι (με) οὐ λέληθεν ἡ τῶν χρημάτων ἐλευθέριος δαπάνη

---

[1] Cobet's note on this passage (*Mnemos.* xi. p. 355) is as follows: 'Supple ἄκλητος καὶ κεκλημένος. Thucydides, i. 118: καὶ αὐτὸς ἔφη ξυλλήψεσθαι καὶ παρακαλούμενος καὶ ἄκλητος. Cf. 250 C: καλούμενός τε καὶ ἄκλητος ὁ θεὸς παρέσται.' The latter passage, *i.e.* J. 250 C, is certainly a reminiscence of Thucydides (see *infra*), but in 201 B Julian has in mind rather the proverbial phrase, the original of which is the Symposium passage above quoted. Cf. Hug's note on *Sympos.* 174. Note too that it has special point in reference to the Cynic Crates, since the Cynics frequently came to banquets as ἄκλητοι. Cf. Lucian, *Sympos.*, Athenaeus, *Deipnos.* &c.

[2] Julian may, of course, have had in mind Isocr. *Paneg.* 42 C. In 234 D, οὔ τι τὴν ἔνθεον ἀλλὰ τὴν ἔκπληκτον μανίαν, he seems to be echoing *Phaedr.* 265 A—the two kinds of μανία.

[3] This is made probable by the fact that, 189 B, he quotes this same letter, 314 C.

ARISTOTLE—*continued*.
καθάπερ γὰρ τοὔνομα αὐτὸ μετέχουσά τινος ἀρετῆς.
ὑποσημαίνει, ἐν μεγέθει
πρέπουσα δαπάνη ἐστίν.

THUCYDIDES.
  I. 118.   J. 250 c.[1]

DIOGENES LAERTIUS.[2]
  VI. 5.   J. 198 D.
  VII. 25.   J. 245 A.
  VI. 39.   -   J. 238 A.

PLUTARCH.
  Amat. p. 759.   J. 225 c : τὴν σύντομον
                                   φασίν, ὁδὸν καὶ σύντονον
                                   (cf. however Diog. Laert.)

  Vit. Anton. 28 : καθηδυ-   J. 208 c : τοῦ χάριν οὐκ
  παθεῖν τὸ πολυτελέστατον,   ἐφεισάμεθα τοῦ πολυ-
  ὡς᾽Ἀντιφῶν εἶπεν ἀνάλωμα,   τελοῦς ἀναλώματος, πρὸς
  τὸν χρόνον.[3]   δὲ δὴ καὶ ἐφθείραμεν τὸν
                                   χρόνον.
  Vit. Pericl. c. 38.   J. 128 D.

The passages here compared may be used to modify the generalisations as to Julian's reading

[1] See note 40 *supra*.

[2] Though Julian does not acknowledge his debt, it is probable that many of his anecdotes were drawn from Diogenes Laertius, as is indicated above.

[3] Plutarch is the only authority for this saying of Antiphon, and it is impossible to decide whether Julian is quoting from the original or from Plutarch. The recurrence of the phrase πολυτελὲς ἀνάλωμα, 103 B, even raises the question whether Julian had either passage in mind.

and the reading of his contemporaries made by Schwarz, pp. 649–653. Of the reminiscences from Demosthenes Schwarz says (p. 651): 'Alle sind der Or. i. ii. oder xviii. entlehnt. Dieses ist auffällig.' Julian, however, does not confine himself to those Orations, but quotes from xx. xxi. and xxv.; his knowledge of Or. xviii. now appears much more extensive than the statistics of Schwarz would indicate. In the case of Thucydides, only one direct reminiscence has been given; it may be used to modify the remarks of Schwarz (p. 650), and though I do not think the parallel sufficiently certain to be included in the above list, I am inclined to think that Julian 17 D εἰς τὴν ἀντίπαλον δύναμιν ... κατέστησαν is due to a recollection of Thuc. 4. 92: τὸ ἀντίπαλον καὶ ἐλεύθερον καθίσταται, or of ib. iii. 9: ὄντες ... ἀντίπαλοι ... δυνάμει.

A noteworthy feature of Julian's style is his frequent use of proverbs. They were supposed by the rhetoricians to give an effect of γλυκύτης.[1] Julian's aim was, probably, to give his compositions a popular colouring which should appeal to the mass of his hearers. For we find that, in his two ὕμνοι, which are more or less esoteric in character, there occurs only one proverbial expression, and that, possibly, a reminiscence of Plato.[2] Julian uses the

[1] Aristid. ap. Sp. p. 499. 20. The list of Julian's proverbs given by Hertlein (Index to Teubner edit.) is almost complete, and need not be reproduced here. Add τόπον οὐ τρόπον (247 B); Σαρδόνιον γελᾶν; Σικελαὶ τράπεζαι (203 A); οὐκ ἐμὸς ὁ λόγος (299 c, 358 D, 387 D); ἐμοὶ σὺ διηγεῖ τοὐμὸν ὄναρ (432 B); cf. Rep. 563); κῆπος Ἀλκίνου (401 A); μικρὰ μεγάλοις (71 B, 73 D); βότρυς πρὸς βότρυν (225 B).
[2] ὕθλοι γρᾳδίων (161 B; cf. Theaet. 176 B); other proverbs which occur also in Plato, and may have been echoed from him by Julian,

TROPES.

ordinary introductory formulæ (φασί, τὸ τῆς παροιμίας ὥσπερ, τῷ ὄντι, &c.), but he more often works in proverbs without indicating their gnomic character. Julian was no declaimer. The extravagances of metaphor, with which a purely epideictic orator startled and held the attention of his audience, are, therefore, absent from his sober style.[1] The following collection represents his less common-place tropes and similes:—ἐπέκλυσεν τῷ πλούτῳ πάντα, 8 B; ὑποτυφομένου τοῦ πολέμου καὶ μέλλοντος ἀναρριπίζεσθαι, 13 B; δαψιλοῦς ἀντλήσειεν ἐκ πίθου, 236 C; τὴν εὐεξίαν περιβάλλεσθαι, 16 A; τοῦ τρυφᾶν χορηγίαν, 16 B; ὁ πόλεμος συνερρήγνυτο, 24 C, 55 C;[2] ἐφεδρεύοντα τοῖς καιροῖς, 31 B; τὸν ἐπιόντα χειμῶνα (of invasion) 35 B; ὁ ποιητὴς τοῦ δράματος (Maxentius), 57 D; ὁ τῆς βασιλείας ὑποκριτής, 77 C; ἀπὸ τῶν τειχῶν ἐναυμάχουν, 67 B;[3] ἐσμοὶ βίβλων, 191 C; τὸν Αἰγαῖον ἀναμετρῆσαι, 254 D; ἀνθῆσαι τῇ τύχῃ, 47 B; ἀποτρίψασθαι τῆς ἀθεότητος τὴν κηλῖδα, 180 B; ἀποσμιλεύων τὰ ῥήματα; ἀποτορνεύων τοὺς περιόδους, 77 A; ἀθλητὰς ἀρετῆς, 14 D; ἡνίας ἐπιτρέπειν τοῦ

are: σύν τε δύ' ἐρχομένω, Ep. 74, Symp. 174 D, Π. ii. 203, R.G. (Spengel) iii. 152. 10; οὐ πόλεμον ἀγγέλλεις, 381 A (Phaedr. 242 B); ἵππον εἰς πεδίον (Theaet. 183 D); τὸν κολοφῶνα ἐπιτιθέναι, 261 D (Theaet. 153 et al.); βάλλ' εἰς μακαρίαν, 333 B (Hipp. Maj. 293 A); πῦρ ἐπὶ πῦρ, 437 A (Laws, 666 A); δὶς παῖδες οἱ γέροντες, 446 A (Laws, 646 A, &c.).

[1] It is noteworthy that Julian never uses the gen. of exclamation with ὦ, except in the Letters. Here he is in strong contrast with such writers as Maximus of Tyre, Libanius, Himerius, and even Themistius.

[2] Cf. Plut. ii. 322 B.

[3] Cf. Aristid. xiii. 259, 276; Polemo, 13. 16: πρῶτος ἐναυμάχησεν ἐκ γῆς; probably borrowed from Thuc. iv. 14: οὐδὲν ἄλλο ἢ ἐκ γῆς ἐναυμάχουν.

βίου, 70 C; γλυκεῖαν ἀνιμᾶσθαι δρόσον, 241 A; ἀρετὴν ἀμησαμένους, 169 B; ἀποδύσασθαι πρὸς δόξας, 197 D; ὁ τῆς ψυχῆς δεσμός (=σῶμα), 198 B; ἡδύσματα παρὰ τῆς Μούσης ἐδρέψατο, 207 B; ἐκβακχεῦσαι φρένας, 221 D; τὰ ἄρρητα ἀναμετρεῖσθαι, 270 D; ἐκ τῆς ὑποστέγου φιλοσοφίας, 262 D; πηγὰς δακρύων, 275 A; τὰ πάντα τῷ τετραχόρδῳ συνῳδῶν, 315 C; συγκροτεῖν συμπόσιον, 308 D;[1] τὰς πόλεις ἀποδιδρασκούσας τὸ λίαν ἀκραιφνές, 185 C; ἀδαμαντίνην Ῥώμην, 326 C; ἀκοντίζειν φήμην, 397 B.

τὴν ναῦν ὥσπερ ῥιζωθεῖσαν,[2] 160 B; Hills surround a city καθάπερ δικτύοις, and a river οἰονεὶ μηχανήματι, 30 A; he sprinkles in Platonic passages ὥσπερ ἁλῶν ἢ χρυσοῦ ψήγματος, 69 B; παντὸς ἐπιδραττόμεθα ὥσπερ ... οἱ λιχνοὶ ... 69 C; ὥσπερ ὄφλημα ἀποδοὺς τὴν ἁλουργίδα, 77 C; ὥσπερ ἐσθῆτα ποικίλην τοῖς ὀνόμασι σκιαγραφήσαντες, 78 D; ὥσπερ ἐς λιμένα καταφεύγοντες τὴν τούτου δεξίαν, 97 B; The sun turns ὥσπερ περὶ τὴν νύσσαν, 156 A; Cynicism like Silenus statuary, 187 A (Plat. Symp.); ὥσπερ ἐκ λειμῶνος δρεψάμενος τὰ ἄνθη (of philosophy), 244 B; A sophist pours out his words ὥσπερ οἱ ποταμοὶ τοῖς πεδίοις ἐπαφιᾶσιν τὰ ῥεύματα, 373 D; μητέρα πρὸ ὥρας ἀναρπασθῆναι καθάπερ δᾷδα λαμπρῶς ἡμμένην, 412 B; ὥσπερ οἱ πελειάδες—σοβηθεὶς ἀναπτῆναι, 204 C.

SIMILES.

Phrases apparently peculiar to Julian are the following:—δρᾶν γάμον, 110 D; γαλήνης ἀκριβοῦς, 25 B, 98 A; τὸ πεπληθυσμένον τῆς ζωῆς, 222 A; cf. 142 B; πέφυκε τὰ θεῖα ... πληθύνεσθαι διὰ τὸ

---

[1] Cf. συγκροτεῖν συνδεῖπνον, Plut.
[2] Od. 13. 163.

περιὸν ... τῆς ζωῆς; λιμὸν ἀλοιήτηρα βρότειον, 370 A (evidently a quotation, though I have been unable to find it elsewhere).

NON-CLASSICAL USAGES.
It seems astonishing that, with all their close study of classic models, the writers of reminiscence Greek should so often admit expressions and constructions which betray either a misunderstanding of their authors, or an inability to keep clear of the corrupted usage of the spoken language of their day. The following illustrate Julian's failings in this respect:— οὐδὲ γρῦ μετέδωκεν (τῆς πατρῴας οὐσίας),273 B. This is against the classical limitation of this phrase to verbs of speaking. δωμάτιον = house, 259 B, 260 B, 263 A. The classical usage confined this word to the part of the house where one sleeps.[1]

The following are the special points in Julian's syntax which seem worthy of notice:

Non-classical or rare Constructions.

OPTATIVES.
Julian combines with the normal classical use of the optative certain non-classical constructions which were brought in by the earlier Atticists through a misunderstanding of the Attic usage, and had kept their place in the literary language.[2] Such are:

(1) Optative in prot. with fut. ind. in apodosis,[3] 28 A, 40 C, 5 D, 88 D, 115 D, 240 A, 237 A, 140 C,

[1] Themistius, 290 D, uses δωμάτιον of his lecture theatre.
[2] See Schmid, *Atticismus*, i. p. 97. These constructions of the optative are common in Dio, Lucian, &c. It will be seen from a comparison of Schmid's statistics with those given above that Julian uses them comparatively rarely.
[3] G. M. T. § 499.

JULIAN'S STYLE AND VOCABULARY 85

182 A, 181 D, 250 C, 290 B, 123 B, 155 B, 157 D, 172 D, 183 A, 185 B, 431, B. *Ep.* 78, p. 605.
(2) Opt. in protasis and pres. ind. in apodosis,[1] 23 A, 134 C.
(3) Opt. in final clauses, &c., following a primary tense.[2] 189 C, ὑπουργεῖ ὡς ἂν δύναιτο. 236 B, ἀφίημι ἵνα μὴ προσκρούσαιμι. 270 A, βούλομαι ἀπαγγεῖλαι ὅπως γένοιτο γνώριμα.
(4) *Extended Deliberatives.*[3] 44 C, οὐκ ἔστιν ὅτου δεόμενος τῷ κεκτημένῳ φθονήσειεν. 94 A, οὐκ ἔχων ὅ τι μέμφοιτο. 178 C, ὅ τι συμβέβηκεν οὐδεὶς ὅστις οὐ φήσειεν. 199 B, ἦν γὰρ οὐδὲν ὅθεν αὐτὰ πρίαιτο.

Julian shows no sense of a distinction between οὐ and μὴ, and there seems to be no method in his use of them. The disproportionate use of μὴ common to the writers of late Greek cannot be accounted for by the desire to avoid hiatus, for while Julian writes ὅτι μὴ regularly for ὅτι οὐ, he not infrequently uses μὴ when there is no hiatus to avoid. It may be noted that while we find in Julian instances of μὴ in every case where οὐ, according to classical usage, would be correct, he does not show the same laxity with regard to οὐ. He never, for instance, writes οὐ in the protasis of a conditional sentence, though this was not at all unusual with the Atticists.[4]

The use of παρά with the genitive as the equiva-

NEGATIVES.

PREPOSITIONS.

---

[1] G. M. T. §§ 500–1.
[2] G. M. T. §§ 322–3.
[3] See Professor Hale in *Transactions of Am. Arch. Ass.* for 1893, G. M. T. § 242.
[4] Schmid, *Att.* ii. p. 62, for examples from Aristides.

lent of ὑπό of the agent is very frequent with all kinds of verbs. It was common with all the later writers (Schmid, *Att.* ii. p. 399, for the usage of Dio and Lucian). Julian furnishes instances on almost every page. ὑπέρ = ἐπί, 24 c. ὑπέρ = περί, 92 D. ἐτέτραπτο πρός, for the usual dat. or εἰς or ἐπί, 27 D. *Non-classical or rare constructions after verbs.*— φθήσεται διαβῆναι, 23 D, νομίζω ὅτι, 192 c,[1] οἶμαι ὅτι, 235 D. In phrases constructed with δέω and the infinitive Julian sometimes omits ὀλίγον (or μικροῦ), *e.g.* 230 A, 242 D, 341 D. Haupt in *Hermes* iv. 30, on a similar omission in *Od. a.* 483, Alciphr. *Ep.* 3, 5, Paus. 4, 17, 8, proves that the construction though rare is not incorrect.

The direct form of the interrogative adverb in an indirect question occurs: 363 B, οὐκ ἔστι πόθεν; 354 D, οὐ γὰρ ἔχω πως·; 6 c, ἀπορεῖν πόθεν. On the other hand Julian sometimes uses the indirect where one would expect the direct form. 164 c, ἀνθ' ὅτου—οὐχὶ δώσομεν; *Ep.* 59, p. 576, ἀνθ' ὅτου τοῖς ζῶσι πολεμεῖς; cf. too *fragg. contra Christ.* 276 E, 238 A, 314 c, 135 B. Julian uses the direct and indirect forms together, 153 B, τί ἔτι σοι λέγω, πῶς προυνόησε ὅπως δὲ ἔδωκε.

The demonstrative use of the article in a clause introduced by ὅς, ὅσος, οἷος, is frequent in Julian, *e.g.* 30 A, τῶν ὅσοι πάλαι γεγόνασιν. 70 D, οὐδένα λέληθε τῶν ὅσοι . . . μεταχειρίζονται. 103 c, τοῖς ὑπὲρ ὧν

---

[1] Once in Dio, ii. 67. 21. Gildersleeve, *A. J. P.* ix. p. 101, has pointed out that ὅτι and ὡς occur in classical Greek after νομίζω and οἶμαι 'under circumstances of especial temptation.' He quotes οἶμαι τοῦτο ὅτι, Pl. *Protag.* 345 D; νομίσαντες ὅτι, Xen. *Hell.* 5. 6. 42.

JULIAN'S STYLE AND VOCABULARY 87

γέγονεν. 169 c, τοῖς ὅσοι ἔπτημεν; cf. 248 c, 348 b.
Cobet would emend 110 A to read ἐγκώμιον τῆς ὑπὲρ
ἧς ὁ λόγος; and Naber, *Mnemos.* xi. p. 406, would
insert τὸν before ᾧ in 104 A, and would read τοῖς for
τούτοις, 125 B, 125 C, 289 B, and supply τοῖς before
ὧν, 346 c. These changes hardly seem to be called
for. The construction was frequent in Plato, cf.
Kühner, ii. p. 459, 2nd edit.; and for its use in
late Greek, Schmid, *Att.* ii. 46, iii. 63.

δοκεῖν μοι 308 B, κατὰ σὲ φάναι [1] 192 c, ξυνελόντι   INFINITIVE
εἰπεῖν 19 c, μικροῦ δεῖν 27 D.   ABSOLUTE.

In the employment of illustrations drawn from   LATINISM
Roman history, and of Latin names, Julian followed,
as we have seen (*chap. I.*), the lax usage of the later
school of Sophists. But he was enough of a purist to
keep his vocabulary free from Latinisms, at least in
the case of his formal writings. Only once in these,
in the *Misopogon*,[2] does he use a Latin word, and it
is with an apology. In the Letters, however, he
abandons this etiquette to some extent. Latinisms
are found in the rescripts (397 A βρέβια and
σκρινίοις). But from a rescript only it would not be
fair to judge, for an emperor is not responsible
for the vocabulary of what is only indirectly his.
Latinisms occur in his private Letters, *e.g.* 378 B
νοτάριος; 424 D πριβάτοις; 430 c ξέστης=sextarius;
376 A Δεκεμβρίων Καλανδῶν.

οἶμαι.—A favourite device of the Atticists to give   ATTICISMS.
ἦθος[3] to their compositions, *i.e.* to bring out the per-

---
[1] Cf. Iamblich. ap. Stob. *Florileg.* (Meineke) vol. i. p. 80, καὶ συλλήβδην φάναι.
[2] 369 B: μυρίους, οὓς ἐπιχώριόν ἐστι λοιπὸν ὀνομάζειν μοδίους.
[3] Hermog. *De Id.* p. 293. 30: ἐὰν γὰρ εἴπῃς, οὐκ ἦν οἶμαι πέρας,

sonality of the writer, was the use of the parenthetic οἶμαι. It was made to express irony, modesty, conviction, and the like. Julian gives to οἶμαι every shade of meaning and outdoes the earlier Atticists in the frequency with which he employs it.¹

Collective singular with plural verb.

Κατὰ σύνεσιν. 19 A μοῖρα . . . προσθέμενοι; 22 D τὸ μὲν λύσαντες, τὸ δὲ τολμῶντες; 24 A ταῦτα ὁρῶντες τὸ στράτευμα; 29 A ἀκμῆτας ἦγες τὸ στράτευμα; 128 c δῆμος διελάγχανον. Schmid, *Att.* iii. p. 93, gives instances from Thucydides and Aristotle, but the construction was rare in the classical period.

PARTICLES. ἄττα (7 times), 263, 183, 189, 206 c D, 348; μῶν (twice) 311, 334; κᾆτα (4 times), 122, 147, 310, 269; δήπου (5 times), 68, 245, 250, 341, 355; τοιγαροῦν occurs in fifth place 318 D. (ὥσπερ follows the word it qualifies, 327 c.)²

Favourite phrases with Julian are the following:— δι' ἀσδηποτοῦν αἰτίας, 18 c, 25 c, 103 A; ἐξ ἐπιτάγματος, 21 c, 39 B, 266 B; ἐπιλείψει με ὁ χρόνος, 28 A,

καὶ τὰ ἑξῆς, ἦθος ποιεῖς. Cf. Schmid, *Att.* i. p. 217; Aristid. ii. 415: οἶδα δὲ καὶ Λακωνικάς τινας ὀρχήσεις καὶ τραγικὰς γ' ἑτέρας ἐμμελείας οἶμαι καλουμένας.

¹ Schmid, *loc. cit.*, shows that in 280 Teubner pages Dio C. uses it 83, and Lucian in 276 pages 57, times; in 270 Teubner pages of Julian it occurs 130 times.

² Most of the above are conscious Atticisms, such as Lucian ridicules, *Lexiphanes*, 21, *R.P.* c. 16. His satirical advice to the would-be orator to learn fifteen or twenty Attic words and sprinkle them into his speeches was not pointed at such Atticists as, *e.g.*, Aristides, who aimed at scientific correctness in their ἐκλογὴ ὀνομάτων, but rather at men like Polemo, who tried by such means to give an effect of learning to a style which by reason of its lack of flow and grace, and by its extravagances of thought and language,

41 B, 34 B; ἐν οὐδὲ ὅλοις μησί, 42 D, 8 B, 51 C, 71 C, 259 D, 280 A; λείπεται λοιπόν, 48 A, 173 D; ἀπιὼν ᾤχετο, 66 D, 230 C, 359 A (this was an Atticism, see Schmid) πνίγους ῥώμη, 23 B, 26 A; οὐκ αἰτιώτατον γενέσθαι, 18 D, 353 B; ἀναμάχεσθαι τὰ πταίσματα, 17 D, 24 D; οὐκ εἰς μακράν, 13 B; ἐκ περιουσίας, 27 A, 342 C.

It will be noted that in several cases these phrases recur within a few lines. This feature of Julian's somewhat careless style has been pointed out earlier in the chapter. Other phrases which are repeated within a few lines are πλὴν ἀλλ'—πλὴν ἀλλ', 146 B; εὔδηλον ὅτι—εὔδηλον ὅτι, 146 D, 147 A; κατενοήσαμεν, 152 B C; ὑφ' ἡγεμόσι τοῖς θεοῖς, 170 A B; πρὸς διαμονήν, 183 C.

τυχὸν, τέως, and λοιπὸν were favourite words with Julian.

τυχόν.

Schmid, Att. ii. p. 159, regards the frequent use of the adverbial τυχὸν, by the writers of late Greek, as an Atticism, cf. Att. i. p. 137 for the usage in Dio. Aristides avoids it. It occurs very often in Julian, who twice has the tautological τυχὸν ἴσως (378 D, 446 A) which is to be found in Lucian and Strabo.

τέως.

τέως was also much in vogue with late Greek writers. In Lucian it always means 'until now,' in Dio 'in the meanwhile' and 'until then' (see Schmid sub voc.). Julian has it meaning 'lately,' e.g. 231 B,

was far removed from classic models. Attic particles, such as those given above, are not inappropriate to the style of Lucian, Dio, Libanius, Themistius, and Julian. Themistius, like Lucian, ridicules the unskilful use of archaic and Attic words, 253 C, D: ὁ λέγων ἐκεῖνος . . . εὖ μάλα ἀνακυκλήσας τὸ δήπουθεν καὶ τὸ κἄπειτα καὶ τὼ Διοσκόρω, οἰχήσεται καταγελάσας σου πάνυ τῆς ἀμαθίας . . .

90 JULIAN'S STYLE AND VOCABULARY

λοιπόν.

and with the forces mentioned above. He uses it about a dozen times, in this resembling Dio. λοιπόν also occurs about half a dozen times in Julian. Its use was frequent after Polybius (cf. Schmid, iii. 134, with references there given to Dio, &c.). Its precise force in Julian is not always clear, e.g. 369 B, οὓς ἐπιχώριόν ἐστι λοιπὸν ὀνομάζειν μοδίους. Elsewhere it means 'by this time' (24 c et al.), 'for the future,' &c.

VOCABU-
LARY.

Specially Neoplatonic words are: ἁπλούστατος, θεουργός, ἀποπλήρωσις, ἀγαθόεργος, ἀειγενεσία, ἀποπληρωτής, ἀποπληρωτικός, ἑνοειδής, ἑνοειδῶς, περικύσμιος, ἀνθυπόστατος, ὑπερπλήρης, τελεσιουργός, αὐτοψυχή.

Words apparently first used by Julian or by him only are :—† εὐπιστία, νεόλεκτος (Theodoret, &c.), † καταμουσόω, † θερίδιον (not in Stephanus), † συγκτησείδιον, πατρόβουλος (Act. Martyr.), παραδεκτός (Cyrill.), † παιδαρίδιον (condemned as an impossible form by Cobet ad loc.), † ἐφυπνώττω, † ἐξαναγεννάομαι, † λυσσομανία, ἑπτάκτις (Proclus), † ἀψυχαγωγήτως, ἀποσμιλεύω (metaph.) (Themist., Synes.), ἔκφανσις (Euseb. &c.), † ζωπυρίς, † ῥομφαῖον (for ῥομφαία), ἀπραγματεύτως (Synes., Basil), ἄπτιλα (Suidas), † πτήσιμος, πάριππος = tracehorse, ἀποτακτιστής.

IONISMS.

Ionisms are rare in Julian; the most noteworthy are ἁμαρτάς, 82, 54, 75 ; γενειήτην, 131.

Non-classical forms or uses of verbs.—μὴ ἔσο (Doric ; cf. Plut. *Apophth. Lac.* 241), 232 ; διαμαρτήσειν, 3 A ;

† = ἅπ. λεγ.

ἀνίπταμαι 154 (Lucian, *Soloec.* 574) ;[1] μνηστεύομαι =
woo (for μνηστεύω) 110 (Luc. *Soloec.* 9 condemns the
use of the middle ; it occurs, however, twice in his
own works, *Merc. Cond.* 23 ; *Tox.* 37), φαίνομαι =
seem good, 281.

[1] K. P. Schulze, *Neue Phil. Jahrb.* 1887, p. 226, affirms that
ἐπτάμην is poetic and is used in prose only by Plato ; (once by
Xenophon).

APPENDIX

I. The Letters

THE Letters published by Hertlein under Julian's name may be roughly divided into five classes :—
1. Those that even conservative editors—e.g. Hertlein —reject. They are 1, 24, 66, 72, 75. The spuriousness of this class may be assumed.
2. The Letters to Iamblichus—34, 40, 41, 53, 60, 61.
3. Those suspected by Schwarz and Cumont.
4. Those suspected by Cumont only.
5. The rescripts. These are only indirectly Julian's.[1]

I propose to consider briefly certain arguments which have been used to prove the spuriousness of classes 2, 3, and 4.

The testimony of Eunapius to the death of Iamblichus and Sopater under Constantine has been the natural starting-point of the attack on the authenticity of the letters to Iamblichus. He tells us that Sopater, the pupil of Iamblichus, went to the court of Constantine *after the death of his master*, there fell into disfavour, and was executed by Constantine's orders.[2] Iamblichus cannot, therefore, have been alive later than 336 A.D. Julian was

---
[1] For the Latinisms in these letters see *supra*, chap. iii. Cumont (*Les Lettres de Julien*, Gand, 1889, p. 21, note 3) also points out certain expressions in them, e.g. τὰ τῆς ἡμερότητος γράμματα (399 A) and ἡμετέρᾳ φιλανθρωπίᾳ (398 B), which Julian could hardly have written.
[2] Eunap. *Vit. Aed.* p. 21, Boiss.

born in 331; no one has been found to maintain that, granted these dates, a correspondence such as these Letters represent could have been carried on. Naber [1] alone among modern critics has cut the knot; he rejects the evidence of Eunapius, and endeavours by a series of conjectural dates to place the death of Iamblichus as late as 361 A.D. His only authority for thus adding thirty years to the philosopher's life is the existence of these letters. Naber does not account for the internal evidence of facts irreconcilable with history,[2] or for the position of the already aged Aedesius and Maximus of Ephesus as heads of the Neoplatonic school at the time when Julian was first attracted to its doctrines, 351-355 A.D.[3] The more searching criticisms of Cumont and of Schwarz [4] have, however, placed the spuriousness of the six letters to Iamblichus beyond question, and it will be taken for granted in the further discussion of the Letters.

It is in connection with Sopater's death that Eunapius records the death of Iamblichus under Constantine. If we accept his evidence for one we must accept it for both. Yet in a genuine letter of Julian (*Ep.* 27, 401 B), he speaks

---

[1] *Mnemosyne*, N.S. vol. xi. p. 388 (1883). It is noteworthy that Cobet in the same number assumes that Julian wrote these letters; see p. 352.

[2] For which see Cumont, *op. cit.* p. 6. The objection raised to τροφέως τῶν ἐμαυτοῦ παιδίων (*Epp.* 40 and 67) does not seem to have much force. Julian may well be referring, *Sophistico more*, to his own writings; cf. Julian, 50 A: ὁ πατὴρ ἐκείνων τῶν λόγων. Synes. *Ep.* i.: παῖδας ἐγὼ λόγους ἐγεννησάμην. Psellus, *Ep.* 6, p. 176, Boiss.: ἐγὼ δὲ τὰ ἐμὰ γεννήματα, τοὺς λόγους φημί κ.τ.λ.; and the celebrated passage in Plato, *Symp.* 209 D, E. See too Gildersleeve, *Essays*, p. 376.

[3] Eunap. *Vit. Aed.* 19: ἐκδέχεται δὲ τὴν Ἰαμβλίχου διατριβὴν καὶ ὁμιλίαν εἰς τοὺς ἑταίρους Αἰδέσιος; cf. Liban. vol. i. p. 408 R., and Eunap. *Vit. Max.* p. 474.

[4] *De vita et scriptis Juliani*, Bonn, 1888; and 'Julianstudien' in *Philologus*, 51. 1892.

of meeting at Batnai, when *en route* for Persia, a certain ξένος, ὀφθεὶς μὲν ἄρτι, φιλούμενος δὲ ὑπ' ἐμοῦ πάλαι, Ἰαμβλίχου τοῦ θειοτάτου τὸ θρέμμα, Σώπατρος, ὁ τούτου κηδεστὴς ἐξ ὅσου. ἐμοὶ γὰρ τὸ μὴ πάντα ἐκείνων τῶν ἀνδρῶν ἀγαπᾶν ἀδικημάτων οὐδὲν οὕτω φαυλότατον εἶναι δοκεῖ.[1] I shall proceed to discuss certain assumptions which have been made in regard to this passage. It presented obvious difficulties to Cumont and Schwarz, for though, by its apparent contradiction of two passages in the letters to Iamblichus,[2] it furnishes another argument against their authenticity, the disagreement with Eunapius is direct, if by this Sopater is meant the disciple of the famous Iamblichus. Schwarz (*De vita et scriptis I.* pp. 24-25) interpreted Ἰαμβλίχου ... τὸ θρέμμα Σώπατρος as referring to this Sopater and to a meeting between him and the writer. He accordingly rejects the passage as an interpolation in an otherwise genuine letter, and in support of this view points out a construction in line 19 which is not found in Julian's authenticated writings.[3] Cumont

[1] The last words of both of the sentences are corrupt, and the first corruption has not, so far, been satisfactorily emended; it does not, however, affect the important words in the passage, as Schwarz points out (*Philologus*, 51. p. 630): Verderbt und unverständlich ist sie aber erst, nachdem mit gut verständlichen Worten gesagt worden ist, dass Julian Sopater, den Zögling des hochgöttlichen Iamblich, gesehen habe. Reiske suggests for 15–16 ἀδικημάτων οὐδενὸς ἧττον τῶν φαυλοτάτων εἶναι δοκεῖ; Naber οὐ τὸ φαυλότατον κ.τ.λ. I would read, on the strength of Or. iii. 102 B, ἀδικημάτων οὐδενὸς τῶν ἄλλων φαυλότερον, which seems less clumsy than Reiske's reading and obviates Naber's omission of οὐδέν, besides having the advantage of a closer resemblance to the passage in Or. iii.

[2] Cf. ἄρτι μὲν ὀφθείς, 401 B (written in 363), with 439 C: ἐμέ τε καὶ τὸν ἑταῖρον Σώπατρον εἰς τὴν Θρᾴκην μετενηνοχέναι προσπαίζεις, and 417 D: μετὰ ταῦτα ἐπρέσβευσεν ὡς ἡμᾶς ὁ καλὸς Σώπατρος; both of which passages must have been written much earlier than *Ep.* 27.

[3] *Op. cit.* p. 24 n., K; versus 9–21 ab interpolatore epistulae 27 inserti sunt, quod probat firmissime οἷα εἰκός in v. 19 adhibitum ... nam Julianus semper (viciens ter) ὡς εἰ habet. The arguments

disapproves of this rather arbitrary method, and is content to ignore the passage on the ground of its corruption.¹ Zeller, on the other hand, appears to take a wholly different view of the words under discussion : 'Dagegen kann *Ep.* 27 (an Libanius) ächt sein,' he says,² 'wo auch, S. 401 B, Sopater, der Zögling des θειότατος 'Ιάμβλιχος, *nicht mehr als lebend* behandelt wird ?' But the difficulty of accounting for an interview in 363 between Julian and a Neoplatonist named Sopater, whose associations with Iamblichus endeared him to the Emperor, would, at any rate, have been diminished for Cumont and Schwarz if they had taken into account the existence at that time of a younger Sopater, son and namesake of the deceased disciple of Iamblichus. That there was such a son is proved by the pseudo-Julianic Letter 40. The author, whoever he may be, writes to Iamblichus and to τὸν ἱερὸν Σώπατρον τὸν ἐκείνου παῖδα; by ἐκείνου is meant the elder Sopater, who had been mentioned a few lines above (417 D). And Libanius,³ addressing one Sopater in *Ep.* 1448, in a tone of patronage, such as the difference in their ages forbids one to suppose he would have used towards the elder Sopater, tells him that he gave one of his (Sopater's) letters to a friend to read that he might see ὡς δεινὸς ἐπιστέλλειν εἴης. ἐπαινοῦντι δὲ, μὴ θαυμάσῃς, ἔφην, εἰ πατέρα

deduced by Schwarz in this dissertation from the use of particles, prepositions, &c., do not appear to me to prove anything of themselves; as Cumont, p. 9, points out, by such reasoning one might prove the spuriousness of the best authenticated classic.

¹ P. 9, note.
² *Phil. der Griech.* vol. v. p. 680, note. Unless Zeller was interpreting some reading not mentioned by Hertlein, it is not easy to see how he derived an allusion to *Sopater's* death from the text; is it because of ἐκείνων τῶν ἀνδρῶν?
³ Libanius in *Epp.* 542, 577, and 1298 may well be addressing the elder Sopater, who died when the Sophist was about twenty-two years of age. Their tone is what one would expect from a younger to an older man.

μιμεῖται. There is, on the other hand, no evidence against the theory that the Sopater of *Ep.* 27 is this younger Sopater with whom Zeller, Schwarz, and Cumont have not reckoned, while its acceptance would remove the necessity of either changing the text with Cumont or rejecting it with Schwarz, and so would furnish another piece of negative evidence against the authenticity of the six letters to Iamblichus.[1]

Assuming that we may safely reject those six letters, I proceed to consider classes 3 and 4, and their treatment by M. Cumont. Cumont made a real advance in the discussion with his theory that the Iamblichus letters were written by one man, the Sophist Julian of Caesarea,[2] for whose biography we rely on the anecdotes of Eunapius and the short notices of Suidas and Photius.[3] There are certain parallels of language and thought in these six letters which seem to favour the view that they had a common author.[4]

---

[1] If the Sopater of *Ep.* 27 were identified, as is suggested above, with the son of the philosopher put to death by Constantine, another reservation, besides those indicated by Cumont (p. 4), would have to be made to Zeller's arguments against the now generally abandoned— and rightly abandoned—theory that these letters were written by the Emperor to the younger Iamblichus. Der Neffe wird aber doch wohl nicht gleichfalls einen Sopater in demselben Verhältniss bei sich gehabt haben wie der Oheim, says Zeller, with reference to the mention of a Sopater in the pseudo-Julianic letters (e.g. *Ep.* 53, 539 c). We cannot assert that this was impossible if we recognise the existence of Sopater II. who could conceivably have played such a part. Naber (*Mnemosyne,* xi. pp. 390 and 342) refers to this second Sopater, but his theory of the genuineness of the Letters and of the falsity of Eunapius' evidence prevents his seeing any significance in the fact of his existence for this passage in *Ep.* 27.

[2] Cumont, *op. cit.* p. 29.

[3] Suidas, i. p. 1007, Bernh.; Phot. *Cod.* 190, p. 98, r.

[4] Cumont, p. 9, notes 3, 4.

But it could not escape Cumont that if the same test were applied to several other letters of Julian, hitherto unquestioned, they would be found to furnish striking parallels with the letters to Iamblichus. He took the step to which his method logically led him, and decided that all the letters that contain such parallels are by this one author, the Sophist Julian.[1] There can be no doubt that here his theory carried him away. Some of these eighteen letters are certainly not written by the Emperor, as editors have seen.[2] But an argument for identity of authorship based on parallel passages is especially unsafe when one is dealing with the writers of an age of Sophistical habits of thought and expression. One who had traced Sophistic commonplaces through Julian, Themistius, Libanius, and Himerius, would hardly have laid much stress on such coincidences as are quoted by Cumont,[3] to prove the identity of authorship of *Epp.* 16, 40, and 61. The parallels quoted are :—

Ep. 16, p. 495, 2 : ὁ μὲν μῦθος ποιεῖ τὸν ἀετὸν ἐπειδὰν τὰ γνήσια τῶν κνημάτων βασανίζῃ... ταῖς ἡλίου προσάγειν ἀκτῖσιν.

Ep. 40 : ἂν μὴ ... Ἡλίου τῶν ἀκτίνων καθάπερ οἱ τῶν ἀετῶν γνήσιοι καταθαρρῶσιν.

But the figure was not peculiar to one writer in the fourth century, for cf. Themistius, 240 C, D, καί τοι συχνά γέ μου ἀπεπειρῶ καθάπερ οἱ ἀετοὶ τῶν νεοττῶν (Julian, *Ep.* 16 νεοττοῦ [*Ep.* 40] νεοττοὺς quoted by Cumont) εἰ δύναταί μοι στέγειν τὰ ὄμματα καὶ ἀνέχεσθαι τὴν αὐγὴν τῆς ἀληθείας, καὶ πολλάκις ἀπέπεμπες ἐλπίδος γεμίσας ἀγαθῆς καὶ ἐγεγάνυσο . . . . ὅτι σοι γνησίους ([*Ep.* 40] γνήσιοι *Ep.* 16 τὰ

---

[1] *I.e. Epp.* 8, 15, 16, 18, 19, 24, 28, 32, 34, 40, 41, 53, 54, 57, 60, 61, 67, 73.
[2] *E.g.* 24, 34, 40, 41, 53, 60, 61.
[3] Cumont, p. 18.

THE LETTERS 99

γνήσια) ἤλεγχον τὰς γονὰς πρὸς τὸν ἥλιον οὐ σκαρδαμύττων κ.τ.λ. Another parallel from the same letter actually rests on a mistranslation by M. Cumont of one of the passages quoted by him (p. 88). For the passage from [Ep. 61] p. 582. 10 : καθάπερ ἀγαθῷ πατρὶ παῖς γνήσιος ἐκ πολέμου τινὸς ἢ διαποντίου κλύδωνος ἀνελπίστως ὀφθείς bears no relation whatever to the passage quoted as its parallel from Ep. 16, l. 10–16 : ποταμῷ κλῦσον ὡς νόθους . . . ὅσα δ᾽ ἂν ἐπιγνῷ καθαροῦ σπέρματος τῇ μητρὶ τρεμούσῃ εἰς χεῖρας . . . δίδωσιν, which refers to the dipping of the infants of the Celts in a certain *river* to test their legitimacy. But even granting that there is a certain similarity between the figure of a father welcoming his son home from war or a sea voyage and a mother receiving back her infant from the ordeal by water, the argument turns out to be double-edged for M. Cumont, for the latter figure occurs in one of Julian's Orations, ii. p. 81. It is hardly conceivable that M. Cumont confined his attention to the Letters only in dealing with the question of Julian's style, but it is remarkable that he should not have observed the real parallelism between Ep. 16, whose genuineness he attacks, and the following :—τοιοῦτον ὃ τοὺς πατέρας ἡμῖν ἀκριβῶς κατερεῖ καὶ ἀπελέγξει τὸν τόκον γνήσιον ; ὑπάρχειν δέ φασι καὶ Κελτοῖς ποταμὸν ἀδέκαστον (cf. Ep. 16, ἀδέκαστον μαρτυρίαν of the river), κριτὴν τῶν ἐγγόνων· καὶ οὐ πείθουσιν αὐτὸν οὔτε αἱ μητέρες ὀδυρόμεναι, συγκαλύπτειν αὐτὰ καὶ ἀποκρύπτειν τὴν ἁμαρτάδα, οὔτε οἱ πατέρες ὑπὲρ τῶν γαμετῶν καὶ τῶν ἐγγόνων ἐπὶ τῇ κρίσει δειμαίνοντες, ἀτρεκὴς δέ ἐστι καὶ ἀψευδὴς κριτής (Julian, p. 81).

There is more point in the citation of οὐκ ἐμὸς ἴδιος ἀλλὰ παλαιῶν ἀνδρῶν ὁ λόγος, *Epp*. 19, 24, and 54 (Cumont, pp. 15–16) ; for though the expression was a proverbial one (see Nauck, *Trag. Fragg*. p. 512, and Julian, 299 c, 358 D), yet the use in the three letters quoted of ἴδιος and of παλαιῶν ἀνδρῶν, which seems to be confined to these passages, favours the notion of a common author (cf.

Schwarz, *Philologus*, p. 638, n. 7). Cumont, however, has not pointed out this peculiarity, and might well have made a reservation here, such as he made in the case of φέρειν ... γενναίως (p. 28, n. 4). In the more striking passages I have tried to show that Cumont is not altogether trustworthy. It is perhaps hardly necessary to point out the triviality of such parallels of language as he has thought it worth while to quote pp. 11-19. The recurrence of single words as ordinary as παράγγελμα (p. 11), δυσωπεῖν (p. 14), οἱονεὶ (p. 15), αἴγλη (*ib.*), ἀντιφθέγγεσθαι (p. 16), τὰ εἰκότα (*ib.*), κατοκνεῖν (p. 17), ἐκτίνεσθαι (p. 18), νεοττός (*ib.*), γνώρισμα (p. 19), has but slight significance for the discussion. But it could be directed against M. Cumont by one who should take the trouble to compare Julian's authentic writings thus verbally with the suspected letters, as I have indicated in a striking case above. Cf. Julian's favourite phrase ἐπιλείψει με ὁ χρόνος (28 A, 34 B, 41 B) with ἡμᾶς γε οὐκ ἐπιλείψει χρόνος [448 A] ; and 240 B : παιώνιον ἄκος with 388 A (*Ep.* 15) : παιωνίοις φαρμάκοις, a striking phrase, and, to my thinking, quite as worthy of citation as μὴ λῆγε τοῦτο πράττων (see Cumont, p. 17). In his use of the latter phrase Cumont hardly plays fair. For the spuriousness of *Ep.* 19 ought to be more convincingly demonstrated before phrases are cited from it to prove the spuriousness of *Ep.* 15. M. Cumont's arguments for the identity of authorship of the Iamblichus letters are interesting and in many cases convincing. Stronger proofs, however, than he has been able to adduce will be demanded by students of Julian's writings before they will consent to the rejection of *Epp.* 8, 15, 16, 19, 28, 32, 54, 57, 67, 73.[1]

[1] I cannot leave the question without a comment on one argument brought against certain of the letters by Schwarz (*Philologus*, 51, p. 626) and by Cumont (p. 20). I do not agree with them that Julian is not likely to have written a letter containing only ' Sophistische Schwätzereien ' or ' Sophistischer Schwulst ' (Schwarz,

II. JULIAN AND DIO

A STUDY of Julian's sources would be incomplete without some discussion of an article by Praechter in the *Archiv für Geschichte der Philosophie*, v. 42, sqq.: 'Dion Chrysostomus als Quelle Julians.' In support of his thesis that Julian directly imitated Dio, Praechter makes a close comparison of parts of Julian's Second Oration with passages in Dio's Orations. Julian only once mentions Dio by name (212 c); there, after relating a story of Diogenes and Alexander, he adds: εἴ τῳ πιστὸς ὁ Δίων. Praechter (p. 43) rightly rejects Weber's theory [1] that Julian by these words intended any disparagement of Dio as an authority. On the other hand, the fact that in this single quotation from Dio Julian should (as Praechter notes p. 43) quote incorrectly, might argue a less intimate acquaintance with his writings than Praechter assumes. His method is to bring together certain passages in Julian and Dio which show resemblances of thought and language, or of thought only, and to conclude from these resemblances that Julian was imitating Dio.

The question here arises, how far is such a conclusion legitimate in the case of any two authors of the Greco-

p. 627, n. b). It must be remembered that Julian had his Sophistical side, and when writing to Sophists was as likely as any one of them to express himself in their rhetorical extravagant vein. That this was not incompatible with sound common-sense and even philosophy, and was epistolary etiquette for Sophist and Imperial pupil, may be gathered from certain letters of Marcus Aurelius to Fronto, notably the following: O te hominem beatum hac eloquentia praeditum! ... O ἐπιχειρήματα! o τάξις! o elegantia! o lepos! o venustas! o verba! o nitor! o argutiae! o kharites! o ἄσκησις! O omnia! Naber, p. 28, *Ep.* iii.; with which may fitly be compared Julian to Libanius, *Ep.* 14: μακάριος εἰ λέγειν οὕτω, μᾶλλον δὲ φρονεῖν οὕτω δυνάμενος. ὢ λόγος, ὢ φρένες, ὢ σύνθεσις, ὢ διαίρεσις, ὢ ἐπιχειρήματα, ὢ τάξις, ὢ ἀφορμαί, ὢ λέξις, ὢ ἁρμονία, ὢ συνθήκη.

[1] *Leipziger Studien*, vol. x. p. 98.

Roman period, that is to say, in the case of men who were steeped in the literature of the classic period, and wrote reminiscence Greek based on that literature? The answer must be that it is legitimate only when a common source cannot be found for such parallels. But even then it is unsafe to dogmatise, for the common source may at any time be discovered in the less read portions of the classic authors; or even in the more familiar fields, a coincidence that has escaped notice in former readings may suddenly strike the eye. But when such parallels can be traced to a possible common source in the earlier literature, and can, moreover, be illustrated from the works of other Sophists, it is reasonable to suppose either that they had become literary commonplaces, or that the writer who used them went back consciously to the original source. This would seem too obvious to insist upon, were it not that Praechter has, in nearly all his examples, ignored this side of the question, and has assumed conscious imitation by a Sophistical writer of another Sophist's illustrations.

An examination of Praechter's citations from Julian and Dio gives the following results. I take, first, those passages for which Praechter claims that the influence of Dio is most obvious. 'Eine ganz evidente Benutzung Dion's tritt dann aber wieder Julian, *Or.* ii. 85,' he says (p. 48).

Dio, pp. 72–98 [1] : ἢ οὐ πολλοὺς τῶν καλουμένων βασιλέων ἰδεῖν ἔστι καπήλους... ἀλλὰ Δρόμωνα μὲν καὶ Σάραβον ὅτι ἐν Ἀθήναις καπηλεύουσι, καὶ ὑπὸ Ἀθηναίων τοῦτο ἀκούουσι τοὔνομα δικαίως φαμὲν ἀκούειν,

Julian, p. 85 : ἢ γὰρ οὐκ ἀκηκόατε Δαρεῖον τὸν Περσῶν μηνάρχην μισθωτὸν ... πολυτελεῖς ἐπιτάττειν φόρους; ὅθεν αὐτῷ τὸ κλεινὸν ὄνομα γέγονε κατὰ πάντας ἀνθρώπους ἐκφανές. ἐκάλουν γὰρ αὐτὸν

---

[1] I give Arnim's pagination as I have not at hand the edition used by Praechter.

Δαρεῖον δὲ τὸν πρότερον ὅτε Περσῶν οἱ γνώριμοι ὅτιπερ
ἐν Βαβυλῶνι καὶ Σούσαις ἐκα- Ἀθηναῖοι τὸν Σάραμβον.
πήλευε καὶ Πέρσαι αὐτὸν ἔτι
καὶ νῦν καλοῦσι κάπηλον,
οὐ δικαίως κεκλῆσθαι;

I give first the evidence from other Sophists that this was a literary commonplace. The same illustration occurs, Aristides, *Or.* 46. p. 202 Dind., and *ib.* p. 257; also in Themistius, 233 A and 298 A; and in Maximus of Tyre, *Diss.* iv. 5. It remains only to give the common source, not mentioned by Praechter.

Plato, *Gorgias*, 518 B : Θεαρίων ὁ ἀρτοκόπος καὶ Σάραβος ὁ κάπηλος.

But the Sophists who used the illustration from the *Gorgias* had another passage also in mind when they applied it to a king in a βασιλικὸς λόγος. It was a reminiscence of Herod. *Thalia*, which is again echoed by Julian, 9 B, and by Themistius, 233 A. It is the famous statement of Herodotus that the Persians called Cyrus 'father,' Cambyses 'master,' and Darius 'tradesman' (κάπηλος).

Another passage in the *Gorgias* (470 E), the famous refusal of Socrates to admit the happiness of the great king, is echoed by Julian and Dio, as Praechter observes (p. 46). But there is no need to suppose, with him, that Julian, who probably was more familiar with Plato than with Dio, drew upon the latter in this instance. The effort of all βασιλικοὶ λόγοι was, as has been noted elsewhere (Chapter I.), to prove that Plato's ideal ruler had been realised in the subject of the encomium; such a passage, therefore, as that in the *Gorgias* would naturally not escape the panegyrist, and we meet it again in the Platonist Themistius (79 A B): αὕτη (ἡ εὐμένεια) ποιεῖ θεοείκελον ... οὕτω διοτρεφὴς γίνεται βασιλεύς, οὐκ ἐὰν τὸν Ἄθω τῆς γῆς ἀπορρήξῃ οὐδ' ἂν ἐμπλήσῃ νεκρῶν τὴν Ἀσίαν.

The reference to Mount Athos which occurs in all three authors was one of the rhetorical commonplaces ridiculed by Lucian,[1] and we need not, with Praechter (p. 47), trace Julian's use of it to Dio.

Nor need we refer Julian's echo of a well-known passage of Xenophon (*Mem.* iii. 9, 10) : βασιλεῖς δὲ καὶ ἄρχοντας οὐ τοὺς τὰ σκῆπτρα ἔχοντας ἔφη εἶναι, ἀλλὰ τοὺς ἐπισταμένους ἄρχειν to Dio (p. 46, 19 ff.). Themistius, in his encomium, has a reminiscence of it (11 c): οὐδὲν ὄφελος ὀρθὴν μὲν ἔχειν τιάραν, διεστραμμένον δὲ ἦθος, καὶ χρυσοῦν μὲν τὸ σκῆπτρον κ.τ.λ.

On page 49, Praechter says that Julian, in his delineation of the character of the ideal king, 'hat Dion stark benutzt,' and supports his statement with :—

Dio, *Or.* i. p. 3, § 15: Julian, 86: ἔστι δὲ πρῶτον ἔστι δὴ πρῶτον μὲν θεῶν μὲν εὐσεβής. ἐπιφιλής.

But in the list of virtues always ascribed to the ideal king, in a βασιλικὸς λόγος (cf. Menander's treatise quoted chap. i.), εὐσέβεια naturally holds a prominent place ; cf. too, Aristides, ix. p. 103 D : ἤρξατο μὲν γὰρ, ὥσπερ προσήκει, ἀπὸ εὐσεβείας, and Themist. 9 B: ὥστ' εἰκότως θεοφιλὴς βασιλεὺς ὁ φιλάνθρωπος. Praechter would see a reminiscence of Dio p. 48. 86[2] (Arnim), where Dio says that the true king values his friends above wealth, in J. 86 : ἀγαπᾷ δὲ πλοῦτον οὔτι τὸν χρυσῷ καὶ ἀργύρῳ βριθόμενον, φίλων δὲ ἀληθοῦς εὐνοίας μεστόν. But both passages are a reminiscence of the famous saying of Alexander echoed

---

[1] *Rhet. Praec.* 18 : καὶ ἀεὶ ὁ Ἄθως πλείσθω καὶ ὁ Ἑλλήσποντος πεζευέσθω καὶ Ξέρξης φευγέτω ; and Maximus of Tyre, xx. 8 : Ἑλλήσποντος ζεύγνυται, Ἄθως ὀρύττεται.

[2] Yet earlier in his article (p. 45) Praechter considered the much more striking coincidences of Dio, *Or.* iv. p. 98. 6 : ἥδιον μὲν προσεφέρετο μᾶζαν ἢ οἱ ἄλλοι τὰ πολυτελέστατα τῶν σιτίων, and J. 203 A : ἦσθιε τὴν μᾶζαν ἥδιον ἢ σὺ νῦν Σικελικὰς τραπέζας, ' zu wenig frappant als dass sich darauf irgend welche Schlüsse bauen liessen.'

by Themist. 266 A and 17 C: οὔτε χρυσίου πλοῦτος οὔτε ἀργύρου τοσάδε ὀνίνησι βασιλέα ὅσα φιλίας πλοῦτος,[1] and it is directly quoted by him 203 C: 'Αλέξανδρος τοίνυν, ὁ Μακεδὼν, ἐρωτηθεὶς ὅπου τοὺς θησαυροὺς ἔχει, τοὺς τῶν χρημάτων, τοὺς φίλους δείξας, εἶπεν, ἐν τούτοις. Cf. Theon, Soph. Chr. i.; Stobaeus, Serm. 214.

The above passages are those most confidently quoted by Praechter to prove Julian's dependence on Dio. In other passages that he quotes there are certain similarities of thought and language such as are natural in a rhetorical composition as stereotyped as was the βασιλικὸς λόγος. As a further illustration of the too great assumptions involved in Praechter's method of argument, I add here certain passages from Julian and Dio, not quoted by Praechter, which at first sight would seem to be echoed from Dio.

Dio, p. 52, 130 Arnim: The ideal king thinks it ἄτοπον Νισαίους μὲν ἵππους μεταπέμπεσθαι, καὶ κύνας 'Ινδικάς.

Julian 50 D: Julian says he will not praise the possessions of Constantius, οὐδὲ ἵππων Νισαίων κάλλη οὐδὲ τὴν 'Ινδῶν λίθον.

Here is a striking resemblance; but compare Maximus Tyr. Diss. iv. § 4: τῷ βασιλεῖ τῷ Περσῶν τρέφει Μηδία Νισαῖον ἵππον, and Themist. 266 A. Themistius says he would choose friends μᾶλλον ἢ Νισαῖον ἵππον καὶ κύνα

[1] There is a strong likeness between Dio's expression of this thought Or. iii. 86-104, and Themist. 17 c. And the passages quoted by Praechter (p. 47), Julian, 83 D and Dio, i. p. 10. 19 (the Phaethon myth), are paralleled by Themist. 17 D: τῶν δὲ τυραννικῶν τὸ ὕψος ἐπικίνδυνον· ὅτε γὰρ μάλιστα αὐτοῖς ξυμβαδίζειν τις ὑπολάβοι τότε ἀπωσάμενοι κατέβαλον εἰς κρημνὸν βαθὺν ἢ φάραγγα κοίλην.

That the saying of Alexander was a rhetorical commonplace might be demonstrated by Theon, Prog. in Spengel, vol. ii. p. 100. 10, and ib. vol. iii. p. 460. 17. Cf. for a similar idea, Plat. Lysis, 211 E.

I

Κελτικόν; and, again, 226 A, addressing Theodosius he asks for what was Lycurgus praised—ἢ ὅτι χρυσᾶ ἅρματα αὑτοῦ προεπόμπευε Νισαίων ἵππων; Themistius, Maximus, and Julian must, like Dio, have read Herod. 7. 40. 10: μετὰ δὲ ἱροὶ (to Mithras) Νησαῖοι καλεόμενοι ἵπποι δέκα κεκοσμημένοι ὡς κάλλιστα. Again, in the allegory in which Julian describes the mission given to him by Helios (229 sqq.), there are certain resemblances to Dio's account of the Choice of Heracles (*Or*. i. 64 sqq.) as will be seen from the following columns:—

Dio, *Or*. i. 64: καὶ ὅ γε πατὴρ (Ζεύς) αὐτοῦ (Ἡρακλέους) πολλὴν ἐπιμέλειαν ἐποιεῖτο.

66. Hermes appears to Heracles: καὶ ἄγει λαβὼν αὐτὸν ἄφραστον καὶ ἄβατον ἀνθρώποις ὁδόν, ἕως ἦλθεν ἐπί τινα ὑπεροχὴν ὄρους περιφανῆ καὶ σφόδρα ὑψηλὴν τὰ δὲ ἔξωθεν δεινῶς ἀπότομον κρημνοῖς.

Julian, 229 sqq.: Zeus commands Helios ἐπιμελεῖσθαι διαφερόντως αὐτοῦ (Ἰουλιανοῦ) καὶ ποιμαίνειν.

280 B: Hermes appears to him and says:—ἡγεμών σοι ἐγὼ ἔσομαι λείας καὶ ὁμαλεστέρας ὁδοῦ τουτὶ τὸ μακρὸν ὑπερβάντι τὸ σκολιὸν καὶ ἀπότομον χωρίον. 280 D: ἀγαγὼν δὲ αὐτὸν ἐπί τι μέγα καὶ ὑψηλὸν ὄρος.

And cf. Dio 86 with Julian 288-84. But we need not suppose that Julian had echoed Dio. Themistius has the myth (280 A) in much the same words as Dio, and quotes it as the famous one of Prodicus the Sophist, which is found Xen. *Mem*. ii. 1. 21, and is mentioned by Cic. *De Off*. i. 32, 118, and by Maximus of Tyre, *Diss*. xx. 1.

Julian himself refers to this myth (56 D), which proves that he was familiar with it. Dio does not acknowledge his debt to Prodicus. We are therefore justified in believing that Julian derived this famous illustration from sources other than Dio's first Oration.

While, however, we may decline to agree in special

cases with the conclusions drawn by Praechter from these coincidences in Dio and Julian, we may well believe that Julian admired Dio Chrysostomus, and even used him consciously. There seems to be a fair probability that, in the following case, Julian had Dio in mind, though the suggestion is offered with the reservations indicated earlier in the discussion.

Cf. Dio, *Or.* i. 9 (Arnim) with Julian, 253 B.

Dio speaks of philosophers as τοὺς λόγους παρακλήσεως ἕνεκα φθεγγόμενοι πρὸς αὐτούς . . . ὥσπερ οἱ κινοῦντες καὶ μεταφέροντες οὐκ εὔφορον βάρος φθέγγονταί τε καὶ ᾁδουσιν ἡσυχῇ τὸ ἔργον παραμυθούμενοι.

Julian speaks of his Greek studies as a relaxation: ὥσπερ οἱ τὰ βαρέα φορτία φέροντες ἐν ταῖς ᾠδαῖς ἐπικουφίζουσιν αὐτοῖς τὴν ταλαιπωρίαν.

www.ingramcontent.com/pod-product-compliance
Lightning Source LLC
Chambersburg PA
CBHW021945160426
43195CB00011B/1228